Love
STRENGTH
Faith

written by
Beauty H. Faulkner and LeRae S. Faulkner

iUniverse®

LOVE STRENGTH FAITH

Graphic Design by Jason Abdeljalil
Editing by Sasha Braun
Developmental Support by Rae-Lynn Whitt

iUniverse books may be ordered through booksellers or by contacting:

iUniverse
1663 Liberty Drive
Bloomington, IN 47403
www.iuniverse.com
1-800-Authors (1-800-288-4677)

Because of the dynamic nature of the Internet, any web addresses or links contained in this book may have changed since publication and may no longer be valid. The views expressed in this work are solely those of the author and do not necessarily reflect the views of the publisher, and the publisher hereby disclaims any responsibility for them.

Any people depicted in stock imagery provided by Getty Images are models, and such images are being used for illustrative purposes only.
Certain stock imagery © Getty Images.

ISBN: 978-1-5320-5285-9 (sc)
ISBN: 978-1-5320-5274-3 (e)

Library of Congress Control Number: 2018908788

Print information available on the last page.

iUniverse rev. date: 10/19/2018

This book is dedicated to Marion Allegretto, my grandmother and LeRae's great grandmother (G.G.), who passed away on July 1, 2012. She was the epitome of strength and a champion of overcoming adversity. We will cherish her unwavering faith and immeasurable love for our family forever.

Essence

Introduction

Hello, my name is Beauty. I'm LeRae's mom. I was named Heather by my parents on December 29, 1964. In March of 2000, I renamed myself Beauty while recovering from an injury that ultimately catapulted me into a spiritual awakening at age thirty-three. I share more about my spiritual awakening throughout this book.

The moment I began calling myself *Beauty*, my life completely changed. I began exploring energy-based healing and became an avid student of alternative medicine. Shortly thereafter, I became a healer or soul whisperer/light activator, as I refer to myself today. I also began writing songs and eventually started my own business through which I produced, directed, and performed in an eclectic mix of variety shows that included local artists. I was in love with my life.

On October 7, 2006, I performed the finale of a show called "The Colour of My Voice." As the stage lights dimmed, I began dreaming about the next production. Little did I know this would be my last show. Eleven days later, my life became unrecognizable, focusing on a spirited, fifteen-year-old girl who until then had been eager to take on the world. She'd suddenly become ill and within twenty-four hours was clinging to life. She is my beloved daughter LeRae and the catalyst for this book.

LeRae was admitted to St. Paul's Hospital in Saskatoon on October 18, 2006, with a rare condition—Guillain-Barré Syndrome (GBS).[1] While she was in the pediatric intensive care unit (PICU), I began experiencing an ongoing, unfamiliar, and unsettling feeling that continued long after

---

[1] A disorder in which the body's immune system attacks part of the peripheral nervous system.

she was discharged. I knew this feeling was connected to my experience caring for LeRae in PICU. I also became aware of the startling fact that only a handful of LeRae's medical staff acknowledged the importance of integrating modern medicine with alternative medicine. Even fewer knew about the healing modality of Reiki. I strongly felt this needed to change.

After the hospital discharged LeRae as an outpatient, I became passionately motivated to do something about my unsettling feeling, and my search for a solution began. I wanted to share the remarkable benefits of both alternative and modern medicine. I also wanted to share essential information about the many healing modalities presently available, which most people are unaware of.

I considered writing a book, which seemed like the perfect solution. The book was to be called "Mystical Magical Miracle," and I intended to dedicate it to LeRae. Each time I sat down to write a story, a song would come through instead. Eventually, I decided to let the book go with the hope that it would return. I recorded a CD called *Mother* in 2007.

I was still waiting patiently for the book to return when LeRae and I had an unexpected conversation one evening in 2013. LeRae had just come home from dance class. Before I could say hello, she asked me to do Reiki on her knees. I said sure and followed her downstairs to her room. She laid on her bed, and I sat down beside her, gently placing one hand on each knee. Within minutes, I heard *I want to write a book* loud and clear in my mind. "Do you want to write a book?" I asked.

"Yes," she said, followed by, "Why are you asking me that question?" I explained what I'd heard, and she understood. My initial thought was a romance novel. I knew she loved reading them and had mentioned, in the past, she'd like to write one someday. I became overly excited, asking her who the characters were and what the story would be. I was midway through another question when she abruptly interrupted by saying, "No, I want to write about my story, my experience with GBS."

For a moment, I was speechless. Whenever I'd mentioned the possibility of her writing a book about her experience, she'd always said she wasn't ready. I realized, then, that she was serious. With tears in my eyes, I eagerly told her, "Awesome, you can do this! I can help you write it if you want."

"Okay," she happily replied, and our journey in writing this book together began.

Originally, she was the lead author and I was co-author, which made sense at the time, since she was the main character and the one who was ill. However, because she could barely remember what had happened, the more she tried to write, the more frustrated she became. I, on the other hand, remembered almost everything. To ease her distress, I lovingly asked her to bless me with the task of completing the book. I reassured her this blessing would free her of the stress of trying to remember something she wasn't meant to. She simply needed to live her life, and I would do my best to fill in the missing pieces. She readily agreed.

My intention in writing this book comes from my deep desire to share information that I believe is vitally important for anyone who is dealing with a personal health crisis, caring for a loved one, or feeling as though they are lost in the abyss of their own darkness.

My heart's desire is to share a profound love story, overflowing with heartache, emotional turmoil, Mystical Magical Miracles, and the whisper of hope that lingers softly between the breath of life and the peace of death.

I am deeply honoured.

My name is LeRae. When I was fifteen years old, I descended into a surreal life-and-death experience that turned my life upside down. Eleven years later, I'm finally ready to share my story. I was a typical, feisty fifteen-year-old girl, who loved being on the go. No one could tell me how to live my life. I was an athlete and a free spirit. I participated in track, cheerleading, drama, gymnastics, and dance. My life was full and fast, and that's how I liked it.

My illness ripped the life I knew away from me and sent me on a profound life-altering journey I wasn't prepared for.

This book is filled with genuine heartfelt stories written by family members, friends, and people who played a vital role in helping me fight through my terrifying, life-changing experience. I'm thankful for their stories, for without the sharing of their experiences and their willingness to do anything necessary to help me survive, this book never would've been written.

My inability to recall my own journey is difficult and frustrating. Flashes of an experience or situation appear to me as pieces but never the whole story. Sometimes, I feel as though the days have blended together and time has no meaning. My journey has been fragmented into tiny snapshots of unimaginable suffering and uplifting triumph. Everything else is a blur. I believe my mind has suppressed many of my memories to protect me from reliving my experiences.

For this reason, I chose to write my story in a diary format as a fifteen-year-old girl moving into my *mind's diary* during the time of my worst symptoms. In this way, I was able to place myself back into the mind of that terrified teenage girl and feel her fear, her pain, and the incredible outpouring of unconditional love surrounding her.

From this perspective, and knowing I was destined to experience GBS, I'm able to genuinely share my story with ease. The unimaginable life-changing experiences related to my illness reside within my soul as part of who I am, yet they will never define me. My near-death experience continues to remind me how precious life is and that I only have this body to live it in.

Welcome to my journey.

One
Dear Diary

LeRae

October 7, 2006

I can't believe I just did that! I just performed on stage. I danced and sang in front of a huge crowd for the first time. It was one of the scariest, craziest, and coolest things I've ever done. I totally freaked out, though. When they called me to sing, I could hardly breathe and started to hyperventilate—there was no way I was getting on that stage! It was totally embarrassing and hilarious when Mom grabbed a brown paper bag from the chair beside her, crunched it, shoved it up to my mouth, and said, "Breathe!" I couldn't believe it, but holy crap it worked. The next thing I knew I was sitting on a stool beside my mom singing my heart out. I finally faced my fear.

Dance, on the other hand, always makes me feel good. Moving to the music is much easier than singing. My dance teacher makes it fun, and she comes up with the hottest moves. I feel so alive when I'm dancing, especially to salsa. I feel the music and get lost in it. I love it so much!

October 8, 2006

I'm so happy and proud of the fact that I faced my fear of performing in public—too bad I feel awful today. I have an annoying cold, but I'm going to power through it like I always do.

October 13, 2006

I'm exhausted. This cold feels different.

October 18, 2006 (morning)

My lymph nodes are the size of golf balls, and my neck looks like I gained fifty pounds. Oh well, I'm going to school anyway. I'm partnered with the cutest boy in school, and there's no way I'm missing it. I convinced Mom I'm fine. Hehe. She wants me to stay home. No way, I'm having none of it. I'm going to school, and that is that!

October 18, 2006 (evening)

Well, apparently, I was running a high fever this afternoon. Mom was right. I probably should've stayed home today. I don't remember how I made it home from school or why I was sleeping in Mom and Dad's bed. Mom woke me up, saying I needed to go to the doctor, but I didn't want to. I just wanted to feel better.

Thank god, I didn't wait long at the doctor's office. My head was pounding, and I just wanted to go back to bed. The doctor did way too many tests. She put weird tools in my throat and ordered blood tests, including one for mono. All those tests seemed silly. I just wanted more sleep. Then I'd be fine. All this fuss seemed like a waste of time. She couldn't even tell me what was wrong until the tests came back. I hate waiting. She said the best thing for me to do was to go home and rest, which was frustrating to hear because I could've been doing that the whole time! She also said something about the ER if I became worse. I don't want to get worse. Sleep will help. I just need to sleep. My mom helped me down the stairs and into my bed—not a good sign. Sleep will help . . .

October 19, 2006

There's something seriously wrong with me. I can hardly see, and my vision is blurry. It must be from waking up so early. Yeah, that's it, from waking up so early. I'm going to school anyway. I'm fine. I'm invincible. I'll hop in the shower. It'll help me feel better.

My blurry vision is getting worse, and my feet are starting to tingle like they're falling asleep. I feel uneasy and off balance. I keep stumbling around in the shower. *I finish showering and know something isn't right, but I just continue as if nothing's happening. Stupid idea. I know I'm in denial. I don't want to admit how horrible I feel, because, once I do, it'll become real, and that's the scariest part. I finally gather my courage to tell Dad about my blurry vision and how my feet feel funny. He suggests I go back to bed and see how I feel in the afternoon. Yes, more sleep, that'll help. I really hope it helps. I'm afraid to open my eyes. Every time I do, my vision is worse. Sleep will help . . .*

I'm barely awake when I hear Dad's voice. He asks me how I'm feeling. I'm way worse. I'm seeing double, and I'm extremely dizzy. I don't know what the heck is happening to me. Dad yells for Mom. His yelling scares me. He never yells. Ever. It scares me so much I sit up in bed. When Mom steps into my room, I try to stand. Terrible idea. My legs give out, and I'm about to fall. Thank god, Mom catches me before I hit the floor. She immediately says, "It's time to go to emergency," and helps me up the stairs and out the front door. Emergency? Why is this getting worse and not better? Why is this happening to me? This shouldn't be happening to me! I can't see two feet in front of me, and I feel like I'm going to fall over all the time. I need someone to tell me everything is going to be okay. I need someone to give me answers. What's happening to my body? I'm terrified, and the worst thoughts are rushing through my mind. Too many things are happening too fast. Help, someone, help!

Mom and I enter the emergency area. I can barely hang onto her. She needs to hold all my weight, because my legs aren't supporting me. She sits me down on a bench and goes to find help. I feel like no one knows what to do with me. I don't even know what to do with myself. I'm trying my best to sit up on the stupid bench, but I keep leaning to the side, almost flopping over. I'm so weak. People are staring at me, probably wondering the same thing I'm wondering—what's wrong with her?

My body is shutting down, and there's no way to stop it. Suddenly, I'm put in a wheelchair and rushed into an examining room. Maybe now they'll be able to figure out what's wrong with me. Doctors are supposed to be able to do that, right? A bunch of doctors and nurses are coming in and out of my examining room, trying to figure out what's wrong with me. My body is shutting down fast, and I'm desperately trying to stop it, but nothing's working. I don't want to accept my fate. I want the doctors to figure out what's wrong with me, make it stop, and let me go on my way.

I can't see or walk. There's no way this can get worse, except it is getting worse. My throat is starting to close. Are you kidding me? How am I going to eat? I can't even swallow. When I try, I cough and gasp for air. I'm forced to spit out all my saliva to prevent me from choking. Apparently, saliva builds up ridiculously fast, and, to keep it under control, I must spit into a little container every ten seconds. What a nightmare! I desperately want someone to figure out what's going on and fast. The doctors order every test imaginable, and none indicate illness. What the hell? This doesn't make any sense. I'm clearly sick with something. Why isn't it showing up? This isn't fair. I want to go home. The final test is a spinal tap to rule out meningitis.

I've seen it done in movies and on TV—a big long needle is inserted into the spine. I don't want this test. I'm scared. I'm choking on my own spit and need to remain completely still. How is this even possible? There's no way. Finally, the medication starts working, and my choking miraculously stops. Dad shows up just before they're about to stick the needle in my back. I'm lying on my side, holding Dad's hands for dear life, waiting for the pain to start. I feel the needle go in and a huge amount of uncomfortable pressure in my back. Dad tells me I'm going to be okay, and I believe him. It's over. I'm exhausted. I have a terrifying feeling this is only the beginning.

Suddenly, I'm surrounded by more doctors and nurses. I'm at Royal University Hospital instead of St. Paul's Hospital. How did I get here? Why can't I remember switching hospitals? I'm lying on a stretcher or hospital bed or whatever they have me on, looking up at my mom, machines all around, afraid I'm about to die. I'm horrified that I'll never go home, never see my friends again, and be instantly gone from the world. If I want to live, I will have to win this war. I choose to live. The fight for my life has begun.

October 20, 2006

My body is shutting down faster than anyone anticipated. I have no control over what's happening to me. I've always needed to be in control, which makes this experience my worst nightmare. I'm becoming more frightened. I'm trying to calm myself down by not thinking about what's going on inside my body. I'm beginning to gain control over my thoughts. Yes, it's helping me calm down.

The room I'm in is spacious and quiet. There are two sliding doors in front of me through which I can see into the reception area. I'm propped up on my hospital bed, which is how I can see what's happening around me. What's weird is I'm unable to fully open my eyes, and, even if I could, my vision is blurry. Suddenly, I feel short of breath. There's a nurse with me. I tell her I'm having trouble breathing, and she left. She freaking left!

I'm gasping for air, and it feels like I'm suffocating. I try to call for help, except no one's around to hear me. Where is everyone? I feel like the nurse is never coming back, and I'm going to die. I don't know why I can't breathe. Are my lungs failing? My fear of the unknown overwhelms me. I'm not ready to leave. My life is just beginning. I'm only fifteen! Oh my god, I can't breathe. No matter how hard I try or how desperately I gasp, there's no air coming into me. Finally, three nurses come back into the room with a doctor, but they're moving so slow! They know I can hardly breathe—why are they still moving so slow? I just want them to hurry. I'm dying—don't they know I'm dying here? My fear is turning into rage. They're taking too long. I'm going to die if they don't move faster. I try asking for help one last time . . .

Two

The Resting Place

Beauty

I fell in love with walking while recovering from an injury I sustained in the spring of 2000. I was thirty-three then, and it quickly became part of my daily routine. I would walk at least an hour a day around the South Saskatchewan River, until winter, and begin again in the spring. What began as rehabilitation exercise ultimately became a walking meditation, overflowing with contemplation, introspection, and gratitude. The more I walked, the more mesmerized I became. The subtle ever-changing flow of the river became a dance of clarity, playing melodically and rhythmically within me as I glided in time with the current.

Normally, I'd park my vehicle near the weir, walk across the Train Bridge to the other side of the river, then to University Bridge and back to my car. On October 18, 2006, I did something completely different. I parked my vehicle on the opposite side of the river, near Royal University Hospital. I didn't think anything of it at the time, as I had learned, through my own healing journey, to welcome change instead of resisting it. The river had also been teaching me to go with the flow. I felt overwhelmingly grateful at the beginning of my walk for my exceptional health, my blossoming career, and all my relationships. I silently gave thanks.

As I stepped onto University Bridge, my heart felt like it was about to burst out of my chest. My body filled with an ecstatic joy that seemed to magnify with every blessing of gratitude I offered. Instead of walking, I began to twirl like I did when I was a little girl. I felt free, happy, and alive. When I reached the centre of University Bridge, my joyful ecstasy turned into a sinking, hollow feeling in the pit of my stomach. Suddenly, above all the other thoughts, I heard, *Something is about to happen to LeRae.* My eyes instantly filled with tears. I simultaneously tilted my head back, looked up into the sky, and yelled, "Please, God, no!"

I heard that same voice while moving through my spiritual awakening, back then, I heard, *You must change your name to Beauty.* During that phase of my life, I referred to this voice as my *true voice.* Presently, I refer to it as my *soul voice,* and I've learned the value of listening to it. At first, I questioned the guidance this voice was giving me. When I did, my physical pain always intensified, pulling me deeper into the black hole I imagined myself in. I remember, around the time of my name change, the agonizing debate that played out in my mind between my fear voice and my soul voice:

> Fear voice: *Absolutely, not—that's crazy! What are people going to think or say when I tell them my name is Beauty? How are my family and friends going to react? No, I'm not changing my name to Beauty.*

> Soul voice: *It's the only way out of your black hole. It's the only way out of your black hole. The frequency of this name will heal you.*

A few weeks later, after enduring more pain and mental turmoil, I chose to call myself Beauty, instead of my birth name Heather.

When I heard, *Something is about to happen to LeRae,* with that same voice, I knew something unimaginable was about to happen to her. I knew I needed to drive home as soon as possible. I spun around after yelling up into the sky and ran frantically back to the van. While I was running, I heard, *Stay calm. Just walk. Just walk.* I stopped running, took a few deep breaths, and began walking. The only thing I remember about the drive home is praying. When I arrived home, I found LeRae in my bed. The lymph nodes in her neck were swollen, and she was feverish.

LeRae had been dealing with a sore throat and a low-grade fever for about a week. Illness for her had rarely lasted more than a couple days, and she always responded positively to the alternative medicine and Reiki I'd been offering her since she was a little girl, so seeing her still ill was odd. Intuitively, I knew I needed to call my friend Tillie before I drove LeRae to the doctor's office. Tillie specializes in a healing modality called BodyTalk. My conversation with Tillie was brief and to the point. She suggested I perform specific tapping exercises on LeRae's physical body and validated that LeRae needed to go to the doctor as soon as possible. When I completed the tapping exercises, I quickly helped LeRae out of our bed and into the van. Our family doctor examined her, head to toe, swabbed her throat a couple of times, and ordered a mono spot test. Next, she suggested I drive LeRae home or to emergency—my choice. The moment she said the word *emergency* I heard, *You need to wait until she is sick enough, otherwise they will just send her home.* Instead of driving LeRae to emergency, I drove home. I carried her into the house, helped her into her room, and softly placed her in bed.

On this night, the familiar phrase "the dark night of the soul" passed through every cell of my being, and many dark nights of my soul began. All I remember of that night is staring up at the ceiling, as I gently wrapped myself up in the blanket of the unknown. Motionless, I waited patiently, for sunlight to pierce through the darkness, as I prayed for a miracle.

I woke with the same hollow feeling I had before falling asleep. I knew intuitively it wasn't time to drive LeRae to emergency. Instead, I reluctantly readied myself for work and phoned my soul sister Doriana, a nurse. She came over right away and stayed with LeRae, while Ed and I were at work. I did my best to ignore my sinking, hollow feeling and focused on what needed to be done, which was impossible. I remember telling Ed, while driving home for lunch, that I wasn't going back to work. When we arrived home, I thanked Doriana for taking care of LeRae and said goodbye to her at the door. I was about to remove my shoes when I heard Ed yell my name from downstairs.

By the time I reached the bottom step and turned to enter LeRae's room, I knew LeRae was sick enough. She'd managed to push herself out of bed to a standing position, but when my right foot stepped onto the carpet, a shocking thing happened: LeRae's knees instantly buckled, and she began falling swiftly to the floor. I was at least ten feet away when she began falling.

My heart raced and the surge of adrenaline pumping through my veins was palpable. The next thing I knew, I was holding her securely in my arms and helping her up the stairs. Ed had swung the front door open and closed it behind me, as I swiftly carried LeRae to the van. I have no memory of the drive.

Ed

"Beauty!" I called when I realized how much worse LeRae had become since the morning. She'd seemed unwell then, but I thought she only had the flu and needed more rest.

"I'm taking her to St. Paul's emergency. I'll call you later," Beauty declared as she carried LeRae out the front door.

In that moment, everything changed. An excruciating pain filled the centre of my chest, and my heart felt like it was breaking in half. I tried to comprehend what was happening. I just wanted to know what the hell was going on!

Beauty

I wrapped my arms around LeRae's weakened body, lifting her into a standing position and pulling her alongside me as we entered St. Paul's emergency room. I placed her on a nearby bench and searched for help. Within minutes, a wheelchair was brought out.

As the nurse gently placed LeRae in the chair, I finished admitting her. The nurse quickly wheeled her into the examining room, and I followed. An abundance of medical staff began to ebb and flow in and out of LeRae's room. Some moved swiftly, some like snails, all with the same perplexed look on their faces, each trying to diagnose her.

I was sitting on a chair adjacent to LeRae when she began to choke uncontrollably, revealing to me the magnitude of the situation. Her throat was closing, and the only way she could stop herself from choking was to keep spitting out her saliva. This task became exhausting for her. She appeared to be in a survival, trance-like state, responding to all the things happening to her, but she was unable to stop the massive wave of destruction moving through her body. Her situation soon became more than serious; it became life and death. I watched her body radically deteriorate, and no one could do anything to stop it.

With each passing moment, I felt more helpless. I feared what might happen, and these thoughts consumed my mind. I thought, is this how she dies? With me watching her? Oh my God, no! I wondered how in the world I was going to be strong enough to deal with what was happening and remain hopeful. I desperately wanted to help her. Terrifying thoughts raced through my mind, travelling through my body like fire. I was so overwhelmed with fear of her dying that I was unable, at first, to hear the divine messages being offered to me: *Close your eyes. Close your eyes. Plant your feet. Plant your feet.* When I finally heard those words, my racing thoughts instantly froze.

A profound peace flowed through my entire body, different from what I previously experienced during my healing journey. The moment I closed my eyes, I knew something incredible was about to happen. What I wasn't aware of, then, was how this incredible experience was ultimately going to change the course of my life. The last thing I witnessed before closing my eyes was the look of terror on LeRae's beautiful face as she spit another round of saliva into her container.

The moment I closed my eyes, my third eye, also known as the mind's eye, opened wide—wider than I'd ever experienced it before. At first, I saw a familiar and comforting image of my inner world, a place I'd visited numerous times during my meditation practice. As I focused on the familiar image, it quickly transformed into something new—my inner world became a soft, effervescent pink. White circles began swirling and dancing within it, gradually transforming into a solid pillar of rose quartz.

The word *love* became illuminated within the pillar and pulsed. The pillar's tip formed a diamond point and, in that instant, my crown chakra opened and the diamond point exploded into the cosmos. I witnessed myself become a gigantic tree of life and my feet became the roots. These roots extended down through each layer of the Earth to its centre. From the centre, a crystalline core formed a gorgeous prism made entirely of crystals. As the prism became larger, the roots growing from my feet weaved in and around it. The words, *Hold here for now*, whispered through my mind.

In the centre of the prism, a tiny door opened into a hollow tube of empty dark space. The space filled with light. I heard, *This is the home of the one-soul matrix.* Here, I was shown an infinite number of unique soul blueprints. These blueprints were all connected to the centre, and radiant, luminous beams of light weaved together like a spider's web. I was guided to follow each beam of light individually until I reached my destination. A vibrant light flashed back at me revealing LeRae's unique soul blueprint, I had reached my destination. I heard, *Focus on this and nothing else.*

I opened my eyes as the inner world I just witnessed integrated instantly with my outer world. What felt like minutes were only seconds, though everything seemed different: the machines, LeRae, and the medical team became a unified field of energy, compiled of geometric symbols, iridescent colours, and complex wave patterns. Everything was vibrating; everything was connected. Even LeRae's illness was vibrating within its own unique frequency. *Everything is in divine order; nothing is ever out of place.*

A gentle sensation throbbed deep within my abdomen. I'd never felt it before. It was mysteriously tranquil and the opposite of how I was feeling only minutes before. It felt like an initiation into a sacred temple overflowing with grace. I wanted to understand what I was feeling and why I was feeling it, to contemplate what was happening, but all I heard was, *Just be it. Be the feeling.*

The message was clear: if I was to have any chance of remaining emotionally stable, I needed to embody this tranquil feeling instead of the terrified feeling I was experiencing before. To achieve this, I needed to consciously choose the feeling of tranquility.

This choice unveiled a deep secret within my sacred temple. It revealed a resting place where a profound soul awakening would occur, and the remnants of my spiritual awakening would ultimately transcend to a higher level of consciousness. This expanded awareness catapulted me into a myriad of extraordinary experiences unlike anything I'd experienced before. Bathed in my own unique interpretations, these experiences have become pillars of mystical insight and answered many of my deep-seated questions regarding the mysteries of life.

Three
Mystical Magical Miracle's

Beauty

I began writing about my experiences shortly after LeRae came home from the hospital. The more I wrote, the more I realized. After I carried her fragile, limp body into the emergency area, every moment became a whirlwind of profound insight and extraordinary revelations.

In my intro, I expressed my deep desire of wanting to share my stories in a book called "Mystical, Magical, Miracle" and ended up recording a CD called *Mother* instead. The moment LeRae agreed to tell her story was the same moment those miraculous stories came flowing back to me. The ones I've chosen to share in this book called out to me the loudest.

Ed

Beauty finally called, and the news wasn't good, so I drove to St. Paul's Hospital immediately. While I was walking into the emergency area, Beauty informed me that LeRae was being prepped for a spinal tap to rule out meningitis. We were about to enter the room together when Beauty was asked to move her vehicle. I knew how much she wanted to be in the room with LeRae, so I waited until she was out of the building before I entered the room without her. LeRae was positioned on her side, waiting for the procedure to begin. I slowly moved a chair close to her and gently held her hands in mine. When our hands touched, she began whispering. I could barely hear her, so I put my ear up her mouth and listened.

"What's wrong with me? Am I going to be okay?"

I instantly felt my breaking heart sink deep into my stomach and my throat close. I tried to digest her questions.

"They're working very hard to figure this out, and you'll be just fine," I said, with the strongest voice I could muster.

Beauty

Mystical Magical Miracle #1

The doctors needed to complete one more test: a spinal tap to rule out meningitis. I was about to enter the procedure room with Ed when I was asked to move our van. When I walked back into the emergency area, a man in the room next to LeRae's was being prepped for an examination. As the nurse closed the curtain for privacy, the man started yelling and banging on the wall—LeRae's wall. The nurse tried everything to calm the man down. Nothing worked. Finally, she called for security.

I was guided to stand directly in front of LeRae's door and to turn, slightly, to face the frantic man behind the curtain. I heard, *Protect LeRae and heal this moment with your voice.* A silhouette of a man suddenly appeared faintly on the chair beside me. His eyes became the only thing I saw clearly. I was in a public place, about to offer a soul song for the first time without my drum, standing beside an apparition of a man, when I heard, *I am his grandfather. I am here to heal the wounds of his past.*

For a second, I questioned what I was being guided to do. I took a deep breath, closed my eyes, and began to sway side to side. I felt the energy of the soul song come up from the earth into my feet, up my legs, and into my heart centre. My body shook uncontrollably, as the song's vibration made its way up from my heart, into my throat, and out my mouth. The man continued yelling and banging on the wall, as I heard, *Sing louder.* As I sang louder, I felt a wave of energy swirl around me and expand outward, forming a full circle of white light around the spirit of the grandfather, the man behind the curtain, and myself. The space I was standing in became hauntingly still, and the yelling transformed into sobbing. I continued to sing his soul song until he was silent. When the silence came, I opened my eyes. I looked over at the chair, where the essence of the grandfather's spirit appeared, and it was gone. When I looked towards the closed curtain, everything was calm and serene.

The door I was standing in front of opened abruptly, and I promptly asked Ed if the banging and yelling bothered LeRae.

"Everything went smoothly," he responded. "We didn't hear a thing."

"No way!" I exclaimed. "With all the yelling, banging, and singing, how could that be possible?"

I noticed a nurse standing behind me and asked her if the room was soundproof. At first, she didn't respond, so I softly touched her on the shoulder and asked my question again.

"No," she said and peacefully walked away.

Mystical Magical Miracle #2

The decision was made to transfer LeRae to the pediatric unit at Royal University Hospital. She could no longer walk, talk, or see properly. Her breathing had diminished, and the doctors knew she needed a ventilator soon. Ed and I waited patiently for the ambulance to arrive. Ed was sitting down, and I was holding the bottom of LeRae's feet with my hands to ground her energy.

Suddenly Ed stood up and walked slowly over to the top of LeRae's hospital bed. He closed his eyes and methodically placed one hand on either side of her head. The moment his hands touched her, I felt a warm sensation flow into my hands and into the tips of my fingers. They felt like they were under a gentle trickling waterfall. I knew the sensation I was feeling was the energy of his love pouring through his heart, into her body, and out into the tips of my fingers.

This wave of love continued to flow between us, until two paramedics, a man and a woman, walked into the room. She was tall, with curly blonde hair and blue eyes. He had a stalky build, with dark hair and warm brown eyes. I instantly felt nurtured by her and safe with him. Ed and I watched as they transferred LeRae's flaccid, motionless body onto the ambulance gurney. We solemnly followed, as they wheeled the gurney down the corridor and out the sliding doors. When we reached the ambulance, Ed silently walked away. As much as he wanted to be with LeRae, he knew I needed to be the one to go with her.

I opened the passenger door, as the rear doors slammed shut. I slowly hopped in and sat down beside the female driver. As she drove the ambulance down the ramp, I prepared myself for the loud siren and whirling light show. There wasn't one. The ride was peaceful, quiet, and uncomfortably tranquil. For the first time that day, my eyes filled up with tears. Instead of cascading down my face, they pooled together, until I couldn't see what was in front of me.

"Is there anything I can do for you?" the driver tenderly asked.

"Pray."

"I can do that," she answered, softly.

I felt her every whispering word weave in and around my heart. A feeling of immense gratitude pierced through the deep hollow ache inside me as her loving words flowed effortlessly into the pool of my grief-filled tears. A flood of emotion descended down my face as her heartwarming gesture invoked their release. I could see clearly again: we were about to cross University Bridge, the same bridge I'd walked across when I first heard, *Something is about to happen to LeRae.* As the ambulance approached the bridge's centre, I received another prophetic message:

> She is already healed. She is already healed. She is transcending a war—the war within humanity, the war within you, and the war within her. It needs to play out. You must call upon the divine feminine through three healers named Tillie, Kellie, and Topaz to balance the masculine energy raging through her body. When this is complete, you must call upon the healers of divine masculine for harmony.

I remember closing my eyes and silently affirming that I believe. This was the first of many prophecies that would reveal how LeRae would survive this unimaginable crisis, and a rollercoaster of emotional turmoil would need to play out before that happened.

LeRae was admitted to Royal University Hospital. Her throat was almost fully closed, and she'd reached a hyper state of exhaustion from the constant spitting of extra saliva. I sat by her bedside, holding a suction tube to her mouth. Ed, desperately searching for answers, looked for someone who could tell him what was happening to her. No one had a clue, only speculations. As I watched and listened to his heartfelt plea, I remember closing my eyes and matter-of-factly, asking for a genius doctor to show up. I clearly stated, in my mind, that I wanted this genius doctor to assess, diagnose, and treat her—now! Within minutes, a male doctor walked into the room. He picked up LeRae's chart, looked directly at her, and said, "She has Guillain-Barré, and she needs IVIG[2], stat."

Though he was confident with his diagnosis, more tests were needed to rule out other possible causes for LeRae's illness, since Guillain-Barré Syndrome (GBS) was rare in 2006. As the GBS rapidly took over, the genius doctor made the decision to transfer her to the pediatric intensive care unit (PICU). As soon as the transfer was complete, her spitting miraculously stopped, her body seemed to recognize it no longer needed to cultivate extra saliva. With this blessing, however, came the heartbreaking knowledge she would soon be ventilated. I gently pressed my face up against hers. The tips of our noses touched, and my third eye connected with hers. I closed my eyes and began consciously pouring my love into her.

Two doctors, discussing LeRae's case, entered the room. The longer they talked, the louder they spoke. Then, one doctor, unbelievably and obliviously, stated, "Her case is rare. If she makes it, she'll never walk again."

I immediately looked up, shocked and astonished to hear him say those words out loud. I wanted to stand up and scream, she's paralyzed, not deaf, for God's sake! She can hear every word you're saying!

---

[2] Intravenous immunoglobulin – A blood product administered intravenously, containing pooled, polyvalent antibodies extracted from the plasma of many blood donors.

Instead, I was brought back to LeRae's sweet, whispering voice: "Is that true? Will I never walk again?"

I pressed my face back up against hers and lovingly said, "No, none of what he said is true. I love you, and you will make it through this."

Suddenly, I felt a warm sensation press down upon my left shoulder. As I lifted my head, I could see it was the hand of a nurse. She leaned in and whispered, "LeRae will be ventilated soon."

As the doctors were leaving, two more nurses entered the room. One expressed the need to explain the procedure before it began and asked where Ed was. I said he was in the waiting area, and she proceeded to find him. Ed and the nurse re-entered the room. I decided to leave. Listening to an explanation about how LeRae would no longer be able to breathe on her own was something I didn't want to be a part of, and I knew Ed could stay the course without me.

I ended up in the waiting room, staring at the wall, when Ed walked in. As he came close, my body magnetically turned to his until we were face-to-face. The moment our eyes connected, we simultaneously wrapped our arms tightly around each other and fell onto the couch. We wept for what felt like a lifetime of suffering, yet it was only minutes. We both knew it wasn't the time to console ourselves or each other—it was LeRae's time. She was literally in a life-or-death situation.

Mystical Magical Miracle #3

Standing alone in the bathroom, in front of the mirror, moments after Ed and I wept uncontrollably on the couch, I came face-to-face with the reality of what was happening to LeRae. The grieving mother within me pleaded out loud, "God, please take me. Leave her."

> *Let go. This is why you practice, practice, practice. You are being called forth to become a channel for LeRae and the Guillain-Barré.*

This was another profound, life-changing message. Thankfully, I understood exactly what I was being called to do. To begin, I closed my eyes, took three deep breaths and telepathically began asking LeRae for her permission to enter her sacred temple. She answered, *Yes, mama*, and I became one with LeRae and the Guillain-Barré. Next, I energetically linked my breath with hers and was instantly shown, through my mind's eye, a shimmering silver cord uniting the two of us.

> *This is the umbilical cord of life between you and your child. This cord is eternal. Your breath is now her breath. Be aware of this always. Keep your energy and emotions in check. This is a predestined temporary soul-to-soul integration fueled by translucent love. Everything is in divine order.*

From that moment, I knew I needed to be conscious of my breath. Did I always remember to do that? No. Was I always reminded? Yes. I imagined that with each inhale and exhale, LeRae's lungs became stronger. At night, before falling asleep, I'd practice ten rounds of Ujjayi[3] breathing while visualizing LeRae breathing on her own. After the rounds, I'd visualize LeRae's physical body in my mind's eye and wrap my arms around myself, imagining I was hugging her all night long.

Ed

LeRae was transferred from St. Paul's Hospital to Royal University Hospital. A team of doctors were waiting by the emergency doors for the ambulance to arrive and more were waiting for LeRae in the pediatric unit. The moment she was admitted and placed in her room, the frenzied questions between the doctors began. I was frustrated: why couldn't they figure out what was happening to her. I began asking the same questions I had asked at St. Paul's Hospital and, again, received no answers. LeRae's diagnosis became like a back-and-forth guessing game.

Finally, a neurologist, "Dr. H," showed up, looked at LeRae, and within minutes diagnosed her with GBS. The problem was he didn't have a confirmed test to back up his diagnosis, so more tests were ordered.

---

[3] Diaphragmatic breathing technique.

Thankfully, he was fully confident in his diagnosis and ordered IVIG immediately to support her immune system.

I decided to go home, while Beauty stayed with LeRae. My hope was that, after she received the IVIG treatment, she would improve. The next morning, when I called the hospital before leaving for work, I learned this was not the case. The nurse said, LeRae had less movement and could no longer lift her eyelids. She also said, LeRae would be moving to PICU soon.

As I hung up the phone, a feeling came over me that I had never experienced. It was total fear. My mouth became dry. I could barely breathe, and I felt like an elephant was sitting on my chest. I began to shake, and my mind was flooded with thoughts, none of them good. My fearful chaotic thoughts continued running through my mind until they were interrupted with, *Call Beauty's parents*—Ken and Carol were visiting Ken's family in Ontario.

There was no answer, so I left this message: "Hi, it's Ed. Can you have Ken call as soon as possible—it's urgent."

I was sitting on the couch in the PICU waiting room when Ken called. I started to tell him what was happening, when he quickly cut me off and gave the phone to Carol. When I explained to Carol that LeRae was gravely ill and about to be hooked up to a ventilating machine, she gasped and said, "Oh no! We're on our way."

Shortly after my conversation with Carol, a nurse came into the waiting area and said, "You'd better come quickly. Her breathing is weak, and we're putting the ventilator in soon."

Even though I knew what was about to happen, I could never have prepared myself for what I was about to see. When I entered the room, Beauty left. LeRae was surrounded by three nurses, who were aggressively squeezing her chest like an accordion, trying to help her breath. One of the nurses noticed I had entered the room and began explaining the ventilating procedure to me as fast as she could. While she was talking, LeRae suddenly interrupted. "Just hurry up!" she pleaded.

Another earth-shattering wave of total fear filled my body as I tried to keep it together. After LeRae's devastating fearful plea, the nurses asked me to leave. I somberly walked back into the waiting room with my head hung low. When I looked up, Beauty was standing by the couch and staring at the wall. The next thing I remember is fiercely embracing her as we burst into tears and fell onto the couch together. When we parted, I had a strange feeling that we wouldn't hug again until LeRae was out of harm's way. I was sadly right.

Once the ventilator was in, the Guillain-Barré seemingly took over. The doctors had never seen GBS in someone so young or to the degree it was showing up in her body. They had determined she was in the fourth stage, which, to their knowledge, was near to impossible to recover from.

Beauty

From the depth of our shattered hearts, Ed and I transformed into unstoppable warriors—warriors for LeRae and our family. United, we individually began our own unique soulful, heart-wrenching journey to do what was needed to assist our beloved daughter in the fight for her life.

I witnessed Ed become a practical, steadfast, grounded warrior, who conversed with every doctor and nurse assigned to LeRae's case. He researched GBS intensely and communicated daily with an online GBS forum to ensure he knew all the facts. He continued to go to work every day, served his customers as best he could, and drove to the hospital when he was done. He informed family members, friends, and acquaintances about her prognosis daily. As soon as he would arrive by LeRae's side, he always softened into the most incredible, gentle, loving, attentive human being I've ever seen. Always kind, always positive, and always steady, he never allowed his fear to become bigger than his courage and never allowed his grief to become bigger than his love for her. These are precious memories I will cherish forever.

I became a mystical, magical, illuminating warrior, rooted in my belief in miracles, angels, and the power of divine love. My primary focus was to stay in the light. This choice ultimately prevented me from conversing with anyone outside PICU, unless it was absolutely necessary. Within PICU, I spoke to doctors, nurses, and healers directly related to LeRae's care.

My routine became hypnotic and robotic. I was either driving or being driven to the hospital or home. While at home, I spent my time with our ten-year-old son, Austin, reassuring him that the sister he adored was going to be okay.

I needed to remain emotionally stable, hyper focused, and in the light so I could see, hear, and feel all the divine messages being offered to me.

Mystical Magical Miracle #4

A few days, after LeRae was admitted to PICU, I transformed Beauty's Healing Haven, a healing room I'd created in our home, into a magnificent vigil. Every item I chose was divinely placed for LeRae. Each crystal, totem, and sacred object, positioned all over the room, revealed what appeared to be a divine blueprint of LeRae's soul. In the centre of the floor, I placed LeRae's Raggedy Ann doll face up with feet facing West and head facing East. In the North, I created an alter where I placed my drum and Buddha statue. In the South, I placed all my angel, fairy, and animal totem cards in a circle, face up. Finally, I placed one crystal over each chakra and wrapped my translucent, glow-in-the-dark Rosary beads gently around the doll's neck.

I united my hands in a prayer position and sobbed quietly, as I set my intention to drum and sing soul songs for LeRae's healing, my healing, and all those affected by her life-and-death situation. On the days I felt too exhausted to walk down the stairs, a subtle, pulling sensation always prompted me forward. The moment I entered the sacred healing space, the heavy, tired feeling disappeared. This was when I sang my soul out.

I have sung thousands of soul songs since my wake-up journey began, each one carrying its own unique story and healing tone. Each soul song flows through me with a powerful healing resonance intended to transcend, transmute, and lift all that is dark and heavy into the light. Once the soul song is complete, I no longer carry the resonance within me.

The soul songs I sang while LeRae was in PICU carried the same healing resonance, with one profound difference—they embodied an indescribable energy that came from a place far beyond the ancestral plane I'd been singing them from before. I've come to know this energy as grace. There is only one soul song I can still feel when I tune into it—the one Ed asked me to sing. He asked me in a moment of immense grief and desperation, after staying the night with LeRae.

"You need to sing a soul song for LeRae right now! She has double pneumonia," he pleaded as he rushed into our bedroom. I immediately hopped out of bed and raced frantically down the stairs. Before opening the door, the words *remember, remember, remember* flowed into my mind.

> *You are lit from within dear child, as are all things, for the All*
> *is in All. Calm yourself and look within. Enter this holy space*
> *with the light within, unite as one, and become a miracle.*

I closed my eyes, directed my attention inward, and took three deep breaths. On the third exhale, I opened my eyes, gently pushed the door open, and walked over to the alter. Everything felt different. I picked up my drum, which rested against the alter, and turned around. I walked slowly over to the Raggedy Ann doll, stopped at the top of her head, and turned to face West. I began playing a heartbeat rhythm on my drum, the mallet barely touching the surface. My body quivered, and my knees suddenly gave way. Another intense wave of energy surged through my body, and the words *Kali Ma*[4] bellowed out from the depths of my soul. I lifted my drum up to the sky as the gentle rhythm morphed into a thundering sound of wild horses galloping across the earth. The faster I played, the louder I sang. I felt like the whole world was receiving this song. Tears of immense grief and mercy poured down my face. As the song reached its end, I placed my drum against the alter, gave thanks to God, closed the door, and drove to the hospital.

"LeRae's double pneumonia is inactive, her lungs have cleared, and she's only mildly congested. It's incredible," the nurse, surprisingly said, as I walked into the room. She continued, "In all the years I've been a nurse, I've never experienced a family like yours. No one sees her sick, and maybe that's why she keeps healing at such an astonishing rate."

I gently wrapped my arms around her and whispered in her ear, "Thank you for loving LeRae."

LeRae's journey with the healing power of music was magical and completely different than mine. Her illuminating experience began after she was ventilated. I knew the chaos, constant noise, and stressful environment would be more than she could handle. As Ed was leaving the hospital, I asked him to bring her iPod and Minidisc player from home, along with her

---

[4] Hindu Goddess

favourite CDs. As soon as I had them in my hands, I asked LeRae by lifting her eyelids to indicate which one she wanted to listen to—her iPod or the mini disc player. She looked up, which meant her iPod.

Before I placed the earbuds in LeRae's ears, I whispered, "Focus on the music and nothing else."

The moment she heard the first note, her body relaxed, and her heart rate descended—a magical moment that showed me how music would allow her to tune everything out and find solace within the chaos. I decided to bring the music from the October 7th show that she'd performed with Saskatoon Salsa. Before I pressed play, I guided her through a visualization technique by asking her to imagine herself singing and dancing on stage again. Each time she listened to the music, she imagined herself dancing the same routine. This gave her the amazing opportunity to practice visualizing herself well again.

Mystical Magical Miracle #5

During LeRae's first week in the hospital, Ed and I took turns staying the night, and slept on the waiting room couch. While driving home, one morning, after staying the night with LeRae, I heard, *Mom, go to Atlantis 2000. The healer you need to bring to the hospital is there.* Atlantis 2000 is a new-age crystal store in Saskatoon I was already familiar with. I remember the owner greeting me from behind the desk by asking me if I needed help. This was odd, since his usual greeting was a silent smile. I remember my immediate response was a tearful "Yes." He listened intently to my emotionally charged words, along with the divine message I'd received, and quickly picked up the phone. Within minutes, a friend LeRae and I had been seeing for massage therapy walked through the door. I thought she was the person the owner had called; however, before I could greet her, another woman walked in behind her. They obviously knew each other by the way they spontaneously hugged. I waited until they were done before saying hello to my friend. We embraced as well and, when we parted, she introduced me to the woman beside her.

"Come with me," she said. Arm in arm, we walked into a sacred space within the store where readings and healings were offered. She placed me in a chair, sat down across from me, gently placed her warm hands in mine, and looked into my eyes.

"Yes, I will come," she whispered.

As we were leaving, I asked my friend, who was waiting for us at the front entrance, if she would also offer healing to LeRae. She was a theta healer,[5] as well as a massage therapist, and I knew LeRae would benefit from her visit.

"Yes," she graciously replied as she pulled me in for another hug. When we parted, I turned to face LeRae's healer.

"I need to assess her condition before I work in harmony with her soul energy," she said adamantly.

"So, you want to go to the hospital now?" I asked

"Yes, now," she responded assertively.

Moments later, I was driving back to the hospital with LeRae's healer. Her assessment of LeRae was swift.

"She needs three sessions," she said firmly as we walked out of the room.

The first session was the following day. We walked arm in arm towards LeRae's room. I was about to walk away when she suddenly stopped me.

"I need you to stay in the room with me and ground the energy into the earth," she commanded.

"Okay," I answered, softly.

As soon as we were near LeRae, the healer turned and faced me, placed her hands over mine, closed her eyes, and recited a prayer. She opened her eyes and pointed towards LeRae's feet: "Hold them."

The moment my hands touched the bottoms of her feet, I witnessed the vibrant, eccentric healer shapeshift into a magnificent warrior of light. My hospital room reality transformed into a dimly lit cave, revealing ancient teachings carved upon the walls. She began accessing these teachings by drawing symbols symptomatically on LeRae's physical body. With each symbol, she recited another prayer.

The second session was like the first and took place a few days later. Things changed dramatically during the last session. Instead of holding LeRae's feet, she handed me a piece of parchment paper she'd written a prayer on the night before.

---

[5] A meditative technique conducted while the client and practitioner are in a theta brainwave state.

"I need you to read this prayer out loud three times and, before you read it, I want you to write LeRae's name in all the blank spaces. This will invoke this powerful prayer's intention to transmute all the dark forces of Guillain-Barré into light."

I wrote LeRae's name down as she asked. I noticed, as I was writing, that my hands were becoming extremely hot. The moment I spoke the prayer out loud, I felt the heat from the healer's hands amplify. I was midway through the third round when I witnessed her hands become a wild blazing inferno. I could clearly see the dark forces she believed were attached to the GBS transmuting into a luminous blue light, swirling swiftly up into the midnight sky.

I knew another unexplainable spontaneous healing had taken place. I remember giving thanks for the incredible opportunity to hold space for her while she offered her powerful healing gifts to LeRae. As we were leaving, I realized the nursing staff had witnessed this session as well. It was clear by the expression on their faces that they were wondering what was going on. Their perception of what happened remains a mystery. No one ever asked me what was going on or who the mysterious healer was. Even if someone had asked, I honestly wouldn't have been able to explain it. This was simply another unexplainable experience.

Mystical Magical Miracle #6

Unexpectedly, LeRae began experiencing frequent episodes of tachycardia that caused her blood pressure to skyrocket. The GBS was beginning to take over her heart. The more episodes she had, the weaker she became. Conjuring up her own energy to fight for her life was near impossible, even with all the outside help she was medically and energetically receiving. The doctors decided the only way they could get a handle on the tachycardia was to stop her heart. They said she was at high risk of having a heart attack and that stopping her heart was the only solution. Ed and I needed to give them our heart-wrenching decision within thirty seconds. She'd already overcome many incredible odds, and now we were about to give the doctors permission to stop her heart. There was no guarantee it would begin beating again. We looked into each other's eyes and simultaneously said, "Yes, do whatever you need to do."

We knew she would want us to go for it, regardless of the outcome. Seconds later, we were asked to leave the area, just as we'd been asked when she was being ventilated.

Ed went for a walk. I ended up in the waiting room with both hands tightly clenched on the three necklaces around my neck—my hematite pendant, a gold cross, and a Rosary. I was desperately searching for the Bible; it was nowhere to be found. I hoped that the simple act of holding it while waiting for news about LeRae would give me comfort. I walked over to the only place I hadn't looked, and the Bible wasn't there either. I instantly fell to my knees in front of the garbage can.

"Please, God, have mercy on her soul, please, please, please. Where is the Bible? Jesus, please, I need a Bible."

> *Dear child, what would you do without the Bible? Without your trinkets, tools, and toys? Where would you find your strength, your faith, your power? Your fear is driving you in this moment. The darkness has come to awaken what you have forgotten. Nothing outside of you can give you what seek. Look within and remember, remember, remember, you are a living light experiencing life in physical form. You are giving too much power to things outside of you. This is the way of the human. Detach from your attachments, dear child, and you will be free. The living light is attached to nothing. Bless everything and everyone with benevolent thought and benevolent love.*
>
> *Your journey of letting go of your trinkets, tools, and toys, including your sacred drum, begins with the book you seek. Give all but three of your sacred objects away, for everything you need is already inside you. In this moment, there is only you, LeRae, and the Guillain-Barré. Surrender, surrender, surrender. Rise from your knees, unclench your fists, and open your eyes.*

A phenomenal wave of energy filled my body. Instead of feeling afraid, I felt powerful, and I knew what I had to do. I quickly laid down on the black couch, closed my eyes, and placed my hands over my chest. I took three deep breaths and visualized LeRae's heart as my own. A holographic pyramid formed within my mind's eye, uniting the pillar of rose quartz, the crystalline core of Mother Earth, and the tree of life together. From the centre of this pyramid, a blazing, radiant fire ignited and incinerated what appeared to be LeRae's present situation to ash. A swirling rainbow manifested from within the radiant fire and the tips of two large wings emerged from outside the flames. Rising gallantly from the ashes, a magnificent rainbow phoenix soared to the diamond point's tip. Flipping upside down, the rainbow phoenix dove fiercely back into the fire, piercing through the crystalline core of Mother Earth and soaring magnificently into a translucent, blue sky. An ocean of holy water, embodying the sky, bathed the rainbow phoenix clean, and the sky and the earth became one.

> *This is LeRae's new life. This is your new life. Everything is meaningless until a meaning is given. What matters from this moment is the meaning you give anything, not the meaning others have given. This will determine your experience. The meaning you choose will either contract or expand your consciousness. What meaning will you give this experience? What meaning will you give anything from this moment forward? It is your choice. It has always been your choice.*

Upon opening my eyes, I knew LeRae's heart was beating. I also knew she was in the process of being reborn, and so was I.

Mystical Magical Miracle #7

I was sitting on a yellow comfy chair in the corner of LeRae's hospital room when I noticed her heart rate slowly descend. This was the sign she was about to fall asleep. A nurse sitting nearby meticulously wrote LeRae's stats down. My eyes shifted slightly and focused directly on LeRae's body. She was asleep. I became hyper aware of the eclectic sounds coming from the monitors and the ventilating machine. Beep after beep, they synchronized, creating a haunting peaceful melody that hypnotized me, as if into a deep sleep, though I remained awake. I could see LeRae's spirit dancing around her body and, at the same time, my logical mind processed the grim realization that only the ventilating machine was keeping her alive. Suddenly, the water tap began turning on and off. The nurse, who was writing peacefully, spontaneously flew out of her chair.

"That's impossible—this is a motion-censored tap. Did you touch the sink or the tap?" she frantically asked.

"No, it just started doing that on its own," I replied, and she quickly left the room.

Have no fear. I am what is named death, and I have come to give you a message.

I felt a shiver of panic rise within me as the warm air surrounding me became ice cold. My logical mind desperately tried to escape the moment, when an incredible peace and stillness settled within me, and I was no longer afraid.

"Have you come to take her with you?" I fearlessly asked.

No, this is a resting for her. I am here to give you a message: whether she chooses to leave or remain in her body temple matters not—I am here for you.

"Me?" I gasped.

Remember, remember, remember. Remember this moment and this feeling for the rest of your days. Hold this feeling within your bones and within your heart. In death and in life, there is always peace. It is eternal. When you choose to live from this peaceful place and from this still point within you, there is no fear, for I am the doorway into the light.

The nurse rushed back into the room and announced that someone would be coming to look at the faulty sink. Her abrupt outburst woke me from the deep hypnotic state, and I instinctively closed my eyes. Tears streamed down my face, as I placed my hands over my heart, offering gratitude for the profound message I'd just received. The icy chill melted away, and the sink stopped turning on and off. LeRae slept peacefully, the nurse was calm, and I was forever changed.

Four
Suffering in Silence

LeRae

October 31, 2006

"Why are her lips bleeding?" I hear Mom say. The nurse answers, "Oh no! It's her braces."

Finally, they figured it out! No one knew except me. No one could see the pain I was in every time they changed the ventilator tape and pushed down on my braces. I've been wanting to tell them I have braces for so long. My lips feel raw and are all cut up. I can even taste blood—fitting, since it's Halloween.

I'm so thankful Mom figured it out.

November 2, 2006

Wow, is it ever bright in here—what's happening now? Oh! It's a dentist! My mouth is wide open. How is he supposed to take my braces off while I'm still on the ventilator? That takes talent.

Ed

I knew the nerve conduction tests were necessary to show the doctors the extent of LeRae's nerve damage. As they continued regular tests, Beauty and I decided we were unwilling to put LeRae through unnecessary pain and asked the doctors to stop doing them. She was improving, and that was good enough for us.

LeRae

November 11, 2006

I'm still trying to figure out what's happening. Mom and Dad are here and doctors are surrounding me. Why are they all looking down at me? I feel like I'm being electrocuted. My parents seem clueless. They're trying to answer the doctor's questions, which only I know the answers to, though I can't talk. My eyes feel tired. Thank you, Mom, for holding them up.

A little close, don't you think? One of the doctors has his face right next to mine, and I can feel his breath. Want a mint? He's yelling questions at me like I can't hear. Stop, you dummy—I hear just fine. He's unbearably annoying and loud. I hear perfectly! Earth to parents—hello! Tell him I can hear! Just because the rest of my body isn't working, doesn't mean I can't hear or think. It's my nervous system that's the problem. How about you fix that? Not being able to communicate my needs is frustrating, because there are many of them. All I want is my voice back. Can someone please tell this doctor to stop yelling?

"She can hear—please, stop yelling."

Finally! Thanks, Mom. She is so polite, I would've said that much differently. Even better, Dad says, "No more tests," after which the zapping instantly stops.

Ed

LeRae's veins had collapsed, and the nurses couldn't find a viable vein anywhere. We needed a solution fast, luckily this was the day that Doriana came to visit.

"She needs a PIC line," Doriana said, adamantly, after she saw LeRae's state. As soon as the PIC line[6] was put in, LeRae's recovery took a big step forward.

LeRae

November 12, 2006

Another IV. Oh my god, enough already. Please, there must be another way. My hands and arms are so sore from being poked. Nurses switch from my left side to my right, endlessly poking me with needles. Apparently, the veins in my upper body are collapsing, so they're trying my feet and ankles. Awesome. Jokes on you—those veins are probably collapsing too.

Okay, come on. It can't be that hard to find a vein down there. Jabbing that needle into my foot over and over is unbearable. It freaking hurts! I guess the drugs are wearing off. I understand this is their job, and I need the IVs to survive, but, my god, this is painful. Maybe they think I can't feel because I'm paralyzed, but I can. I want to tell then I can feel every single needle, but I have no way to do that, so I continue suffering in silence.

Doriana has just walked into my room. She looks at me and says, "Why doesn't she have a PIC line yet?" and left. Well, hello to you too.

November 14, 2006

I'm being prepped for surgery. Apparently, it's pretty serious, and they have to put me under. Why is this such a big deal? Whatever. I'll do anything to get rid of those damn needles.

I'm awake and out of surgery. There's a bandage covering something on my upper right arm. The nurse says, "This is a PIC line—one IV for all of your medications." Shut the front door! No freaking way! Yahoo! This is amazing! I could just jump out of bed! Oh, wait—oops, I can't. At least I don't have to suffer the endless poking anymore. Thanks, Dori!

---

[6] Peripherally inserted central catheter

Ed

Watching LeRae go through all those horrific challenges was an experience beyond words. Yet, even with everything she faced and everything she was dealing with, she was also recovering at a miraculous rate.

I remember leaving the hospital every evening, while she remained in PICU, and feeling totally exhausted as I made my way across the never-ending parking lot to my vehicle. While at home, I spent time with Austin, went to bed, and woke up early the next morning. My first call was always to the hospital to see how LeRae's night was, then I'd drive to work and back to the hospital. This routine seemed to last forever. I remember thinking that my experience was nothing compared to what LeRae was dealing with. Her strength, courage, and will power kept me going through the never-ending meetings with numerous doctors. Beauty decided, after the third meeting, that she was done participating. She said her primary focus would be to stay in the light and away from the energy of the grim prognoses we were continuously being given. I understood exactly where she was coming from and assured her I would have no problem attending the meetings without her since most of them were follow-ups anyway.

Two meetings standout. I clearly remember the meeting I was called to with a new male doctor who had been assigned to LeRae's case shortly after she was ventilated. He asked a nurse to join us, which I thought was odd, until I looked into her eyes. I knew then that the only reason she was there was to help me take the news. The doctor started the meeting by explaining what his books told him about stage-four GBS and that the outcome was unknown. He also explained how her nerves were being attacked by her immune system. He was mid-sentence, saying, "She may not—," when I interrupted: "I'm sorry, but you don't know my daughter. She's a fighter, and she's going to write a new chapter in your medical book!"

The look on his face said it all. Thankfully, the nurse who joined us tagged on to my positive statement. After this, the meeting took on a whole different feel. It went from what we don't know to what was the best way to help LeRae.

The second memorable meeting was with another new doctor assigned to LeRae's case. He called me in to an urgent meeting. He believed he'd found an answer other than the GBS diagnosis.

"We have a breakthrough, and we found out what the problem is—it's porphyria," he said, confidently.

Porphyria[7] had been high on the list of diagnoses among all doctors when LeRae first arrived at Royal University Hospital. I knew, to diagnose her, a positive test needed to confirm it.

"Do you have a positive test?" I curiously asked him.

"No, however, there was an abnormality in her test results," he reluctantly said. "All the signs are pointing in that direction since LeRae isn't responding to the first round of IVIG."

Before he could say another word, I interrupted him. "Have you checked with the resident doctor who happens to be from South Africa?"

"No."

"Well, I had a conversation with him, and he told me porphyria is well-known in South Africa. He also said he would eat his shorts if it was porphyria."

A blank stare came over the doctor's face. "I will look into it," he said awkwardly as he closed the file.

We didn't hear about porphyria again until the other doctor assigned to LeRae's case walked into her room. Beauty was standing beside LeRae's bed, and I was standing in the corner of the room. We were surprised to see the doctor, because she had already checked on LeRae earlier that day.

"The final test results came back, and it's not porphyria. The previous test was a false positive," the doctor said joyfully.

Before LeRae and I had a chance to say anything, Beauty started doing her happy dance, jumping for joy and flapping her arms up and down like she was about to fly away. Beauty was ecstatic, because, until then, all LeRae's medications needed to be checked against a list of compatible medications, to ensure she didn't have an adverse reaction to the nerve pain medication she was taking. A simple thing like Tums, to alleviate LeRae's heartburn, could have negatively affected her recovery. Finding out that the test was a false positive was a major relief and meant LeRae was no longer under any restrictions. Her access to all medications lessened everyone's stress.

---

[7] A rare hereditary disease in which the blood pigment hemoglobin is abnormally metabolized.

The best part was the ripple effect Beauty's happy dance had on the female doctor. As soon as Beauty started jumping up and down, the doctor began jumping up and down with her, even flapping her arms! It was awesome to witness their joyful exchange and see the look on the doctor's face when she realized what she was doing.

Five
Triage

Beauty

After receiving the message, *You must call upon the divine feminine through three healers named Tillie, Kellie, and Topaz to balance the masculine energy raging through her body,* I knew I needed to act quickly. I also knew that to hold the energy of this intimate soul-to-soul triage, the divine feminine had to be in female form and the divine masculine in male form, even though the divine feminine and divine masculine have nothing to do with gender. As soon as I was near a phone, I called Topaz and Kellie (Tillie was already involved). Kellie, Topaz, and Tillie began working with LeRae, simultaneously and distantly, invoking the divine feminine trinity of light, love, and compassion into action.

Topaz was unwavering in her commitment to do whatever she could to assist LeRae and our family through our terrifying life-changing experience. The moment she heard news of LeRae's life-and-death circumstance, she began devoting hours of her time, offering distant healing. She also visited LeRae in the wee hours of the morning before going to work to ensure LeRae was receiving as much Reiki as possible. LeRae doesn't remember Topaz visiting her, but she does recall the warmth of Topaz's healing hands on her face, stomach, and feet.

Each time Topaz and I spoke on the phone, I could hear the heartbreak in her voice as she offered deeper insight regarding LeRae's health crisis. One conversation stands out: LeRae was in PICU, fighting through another infection. I had descended briefly into the grieving mother within and needed to talk to someone. I called Topaz. She listened patiently to my grief-filled words: "Why is this happening? Why, why, why?"

"Thy will be done, Beauty. Thy will be done."

A sobering silence fell over our conversation.

I felt the depth of her words flow through me, as I heard, *No one gets a free pass, dear one, no one.* Without saying a word, I gently hung up the phone.

Topaz continued to visit LeRae until she was transferred to City Hospital. She also continued offering the two of us distant healing long after LeRae came home from the hospital. She often said she could feel me more than she could feel LeRae, and that I needed to receive the energy as well. She was right.

Tillie and I met during my spiritual awakening. I began seeing her for healing sessions, and we became friends. Eventually, LeRae became Tillie's client as well, seeing her for massage and BodyTalk, to assist with issues that were bothering her.

Tillie

LeRae, with Beauty, came to see me for a few sessions prior to her performance, regarding a rash that was bothering her and her fear of singing in public. The first two BodyTalk sessions addressed her rash. One of the reasons for her rash was her sensitivity to tomatoes, so I encouraged her to stop consuming foods with a tomato base to see if the rash cleared up. The next session was a performance agenda to work on her fear of singing in public. This session highlighted the two previous sessions and connected her rash to her fear. In hindsight, I now understand her body already knew that the GBS was going to happen, and that this was why the performance agenda was a priority for LeRae before the show. I experienced a foreboding feeling near the end of the performance-agenda session, when the rash, tomatoes, and public singing connection became apparent through a big energy surrounding the actual event.

The next time I saw LeRae was the night of the October 7th show. I was sitting with my two daughters and granddaughter, enjoying all the performances. Then it was time for LeRae to sing with Beauty. They sang "Angel," by Sarah McLachlan. When LeRae started to sing, I became completely immersed in the same foreboding feeling I had at the end of our sessions together. I thought the performance agenda was done, but all I could feel were unresolved feelings related to the links I had received and had not followed. I was uncertain of what to do with the information LeRae's body had given me.

I noticed that the family members I had brought were all staring at me. One of my daughters said, "Mom, do you feel that?"

We all looked back at the stage, then back at each other, as the song finished. They wanted to leave. I knew there was only one more act, so we stayed. As soon as the lights came up, all three girls said, "We need to go now," and we left.

On the way to the car, no one spoke. As soon as we jumped into the vehicle, the same daughter who'd spoken up before said, "It felt like something bad was going to happen."

I answered, "I know. I felt it too. We should pray, like in the arms of an Angel."

We were all affected by LeRae's performance. I believe our prayers we were already contributing to a good outcome, even before the GBS happened.

One-week later, Beauty called me. I told her to take LeRae to the doctor or emergency. I no longer had the foreboding feeling, more like whatever was going to happen was already happening, and I couldn't see the outcome. The next time I spoke to Beauty, LeRae was about to be put on the ventilator. I remember hearing the fear in Beauty's voice when she told me we should treat her alternatively, because she, at the time, believed more in the healing benefits of alternative medicine than in modern medicine. However, I instantly responded with "Western medicine can do for her what we can't, right now," and told her I would focus on LeRae, the family, and anyone working with her during her recovery. I encouraged Beauty to trust herself and reassured her that she was in the right place. When I hung up the telephone, I suddenly had the shivers. They were related to the first session I did for Ed, weeks earlier, about opening his heart. The message that came through during that session was that he was going to experience having his heart ripped open and to be more vulnerable to love his family more fully—I wasn't shown how. All I remember was my feeling during his session and teasing him afterward by saying, "It is going to be big Ed. It is going to be big!"

He didn't seem phased by my teasing, and I didn't see him again until the night of the show. Realizing how the message I had received was playing out, my heart went out to him with a deeper understanding of what his session meant.

During sessions, I receive signs and symbols, but they don't normally stick with me. However, this drama was starting to play out in slow motion, starting with LeRae's sessions weeks earlier and I began questioning my part in this drama.

A few weeks passed by, and I received another call from Beauty. She asked if I would come to the hospital and work on LeRae. All I remember is sitting in my vehicle, in the hospital parking lot, crying. My partner Alvin was calling me to see where I was, because Beauty was calling him, and all I was trying to do was compose myself. The fear I again heard in Beauty's voice touched me deeply. The mother in her was connecting with the mother in me, and my heart was breaking for her. I realized this family was more than clients; they had become my friends, and I wanted to do whatever I could to help. This was when I received the program I would use while working with LeRae, and my emotions were the catalyst that allowed me to receive it more effectively.

I made my way up to PICU. Beauty was standing with a doctor, who was just about to leave. I stopped him and asked, "What do you think it is?" He was confident that it was GBS. I asked him what happens during the progression of this disease, and he explained it to me. I also asked him what signs the body would show when it was recovering and what he would look for first. I continued to ask him questions, until I was clear. After talking to him, I was relieved and no longer scared about my role in LeRae's recovery.

The information he gave me became the template I focused on while treating LeRae, both at the hospital and distantly. I was confident that, with this new information, I could speed up her recovery by also using PaRama BodyTalk, with which I could come up with timelines.

The following night, I used a mindscape technique with LeRae (mindscape is like putting on the skin of someone else), and I was able to communicate with her to find out what her body needed. She guided me to the areas that needed work, and I used this technique until she was off life support. With this technique, I was able to be right there with her, having ongoing conversations. She seemed to be in a tunnel, and I was talking to her from the other side, soothing her and asking her to stay calm.

I remember a couple of key sessions I had with LeRae at the hospital. During the first one, I was treating her right foot and leg. The second included helping LeRae to develop and awaken a yes-or-no response system.

I remember visiting LeRae shortly after the session and Beauty telling me how she was communicating with LeRae through eye signals that indicated *yes* and *no*. Her eyelids needed to be lifted first, which allowed her to look up for yes and down for no. Some nurses and doctors were still treating LeRae as if she was unconscious, like she was unaware of what was happening around her. In fact, I have a clear memory of Beauty sharing LeRae's yes-and-no responses with me when a doctor interrupted our conversation, and blatantly said, "Don't get your hopes up—she may be like this for a year before she wakes up. Then it will likely take another year for her to walk again." He told us she could not possibly be communicating at this point. Beauty gave me a look that said, *Just ignore him; he doesn't know what he's talking about.* She then proceeded to show me how LeRae communicated. She lifted LeRae's eyelid and asked her some yes-and-no questions, which LeRae answered correctly, without hesitation—a clear sign LeRae was healing.

Beauty

I have also known Kellie for many years. We had facilitated workshops together, which gave us the opportunity to cultivate a beautiful friendship. In her own words, Kellie shares her experience with LeRae and the GBS.

Kellie

I have what I like to call a *heart connection* with LeRae's mom, Beauty. This loving connection, for me, includes trust and non-judgemental, unconditional caring and is also the kind of connection that preludes words—some call it telepathy. It is more than that, though. It is a communication through which parallel and synchronistic events occur. When LeRae was starting her journey with the entity known as GBS (whom I refer to as Gil), and before I was consciously aware of it, I intuitively knew something was coming my way. I started preparing my body with better nutrition and more rest. I remember, while I was preparing my body for the drama that was about to unfold, all the personal drama I was in at the time just fell away, and I was able to surrender to the unknown. LeRae's journey of paralysis created sadness, fear, anger, and love within me. All the emotions that I can feel emerged in full force.

For me, a spiritual action takes form when I listen to what I call my *heart voice* or *higher self* and go into my sacred heart space—that peaceful meditative space within me, where truth, trust, and love reside, and my mind, body, and spirit settle in. I remember seeing LeRae, a few weeks before her journey began, sitting beautifully poised on a stool on stage with her mother sitting beside her. They were singing a touching Sarah McLachlan song, called "Angel," which, at the time, brought tears to my eyes and does again now as I type these words.

When Gil came to visit LeRae, the question many of us had was why her? She was a healthy, vibrant, young lady, a gymnast, a dancer, and so much more. I would say this is exactly why Gil visited her.

I believe Spirit will never give us anything we are unable to handle. It became clear to me that LeRae's heroic journey would positively affect many people, including myself.

As a visual person on a shamanic path, I can journey to other realms with "sight," while being guided as to my purpose there. During my shamanic healing journeys with LeRae, I could see places in her body that were blocked, or I could see various colours, images, etc., that would guide me to where I needed to focus my energy. I would set my intentions to allow loving, healing, universal energy to flow through me, as if I were a hollow tube that would transmit to LeRae. Sometimes, I would see and feel the magnificence of light, along with other healers holding healing energy for her as well. To have witnessed such endless and formless power was and is a highly charged emotional feeling. During this time in LeRae's life, many healers, including myself, were called in to come and work together as one, without separation or judgement.

I remember, weeks into LeRae's healing, thinking about a familiar pain in my right leg, which I had labeled as being from a certain situation in my life. As I journeyed into the pain, I was to let go of the label I had placed on the pain and allow new information to surface. I surrendered, yet again, and went on with my day. Later, I had a need to go for massage and have my right leg worked on. Of course, my massage therapist (whom I, importantly, deeply trust) happened to have an appointment available. When I relaxed, the energy moving in my right leg became very strong. I journeyed into the pain again and asked what the message was: it was Gil communicating with me. My emotions flooded my body, and I accepted this presence without fear. The message was clear. The entity was sad and wanted me to know that it was both light and dark, and that it has carried human anger and pain within its own energy for a long time. I cried long and hard as I felt the pain of this entity, while my therapist held space for me. I shared this message with others, particularly Beauty, as I was guided to, and now these words are on paper.

For me the message was clear: all beings, all entities, want to be accepted and loved unconditionally, even the shadow side. I believe every journey has a gift for everyone, including myself. Perhaps the heart connection I have with Beauty and the healing work I was called to do with LeRae represent a goal I should reach for with all beings—a goal, I feel, we can all move towards in harmony. I also believe when we choose to live life guided by our hearts, the abundance of universal love and support is unending. This, to me, is spiritual healing. We can all access it. We can all live it.

Beauty

You must call upon the healers of divine masculine for harmony.

My first call was to my friend Trent, who is a shaman. When I shared LeRae's health crisis, he immediately said, "I've already been on it. LeRae called me in." He also said he would continue working with her distantly until he was no longer needed.

Trent

My name is Trent Deerhorn. I am a twenty-first century shaman in the Saskatoon area. LeRae is the daughter of my dear friend Beauty. When I was first asked to contribute to the story of LeRae's recovery, I immediately agreed and then instantly panicked—the events of LeRae's recovery had happened a while back, and I wasn't sure if I would remember my entire experience working with LeRae accurately. Beauty reminded me of a few things, which jogged my memory quite efficiently.

When I received LeRae's telepathic call, and after talking to Beauty on the phone about LeRae's sudden life-threatening illness, I immediately wanted to help in whatever way I could. For me, that meant a lot of things. I am a shaman who offers an abundance of healing and ceremonial work for the purpose of helping people find their way in life and to heal their old wounds. This may include energy healing, either with the person in front of me or over a long distance. The idea is to help release blocked energy and promote the flow of fresh Universal healing energy through the system, which then helps maintain a state of balance and flow of energy for the individual. In part, I am a bit of an energy technician and, in part, I am also connected to Spirit, which directs what is to be done. I listen carefully to the guidance that Spirit has to offer while working with energy. I also do my best to get out of Spirit's way while it does its work!

When I first heard about the health challenges LeRae was experiencing, the first thing I did was light a candle, dedicate that candle to LeRae's healing, and launch several prayers for LeRae's healing up to Spirit. I did that every single day while LeRae was in the hospital, because, when someone is on my healing "hit list," I am persistent and unwavering. In fact, if that candle should burn out part way through the day, I light another, and if the candle should burn out in the middle of the night, I immediately wake up and light another. I am a bit like a pit bull that way. Once I latch onto a purpose and an outcome, I don't let go until it is accomplished.

Why a candle? Fire is the element of Spirit and instant change. The use of a candle for connection with Spirit is in almost every culture. The saying, "It is far better to light a candle than it is to curse the darkness," sums it up perfectly.

When the time came to do soul retrieval work for LeRae, I sensed she was detaching from her body/temple and that she did not want to come back. I journeyed to where she was through the dream weave, which connects all things throughout time and space in all dimensions of all universal levels. I found her laughing and having fun with a young woman with reddish brown hair. This woman was quite tall and had a childlike demeanor. They were in a meadow, singing and dancing to tinkling music. As I approached, the woman indicated to LeRae that I had arrived. LeRae knew who I was; however, she didn't want to come back to her human existence, as it frightened her and was painful. I explained that the only reason I was able to come to her in this place was that Spirit knew she wasn't finished with what she had come to do, and had sent me to find her and bring her home. She cried and held onto the tall woman. The woman gave me a knowing smile and tilted LeRae's face up to her own. She said she would be here in this place anytime LeRae wanted to visit, but that LeRae must go home and finish her work. If she stayed, she would simply have to redo the whole thing in another incarnation. I said it was usually easier to just do the work once and get it over with, than to come back time and time again for a redo. LeRae was sad, but let the woman go. She turned to me and asked, "How do we get back?" I took her hand and travelled back to her hospital room. As we were coming in for a landing, LeRae was happy to see her mom. She was sad that her mom was so sad. I told her this was an opportunity for Beauty to experience her own abundance of inner strength and, with that strength, LeRae would be alright, because it was all being given to her to help her heal. LeRae asked me if she was going to survive this ordeal. I told her this was up to her, and that she had a lot of friends and family rooting for her. Without delay, she slipped back into her body/temple. When I shared this story with Beauty, she said, "Of course! That was my Aunt Carol!" and the identity of the tall woman was understood.

One day, as I was getting ready to head out the door for a road trip to Edmonton, the phone rang. Instantly, I knew I had unresolved issues with the woman who was calling and was hesitant to take the call. When she told me that Beauty had asked the two of us to journey together, to help LeRae, I knew my experience was going to become more personally challenging. We decided to set our differences aside but had to wait to do the work until I was available in Edmonton. From my Edmonton hotel room, I joined forces with her in Saskatoon, and we did a journey for LeRae distantly. During this journey I was able to introduce LeRae to a new Spirit Guide sent to help her with her health challenge.

It took LeRae many months to heal from her ordeal. I, as well as many other friends and family, were quite relieved she did.

Beauty

Alvin, who is Tillie's partner, was also called in to assist LeRae. They share their stories.

Alvin

I first heard about LeRae's illness through Tillie. I instantly offered LeRae a prayer and another one before I fell asleep that night. I had a dream. In my dream, a visitor, a Dene[8] Elder with blue eyes dressed in tanned leather, was saying something, but I couldn't understand him. Images of my conversation with LeRae's father earlier that day flashed by, and I could feel LeRae's energy. She was in pain. I woke the following morning, knowing I was meant to help LeRae, and decided to go to the hospital with Tillie. I was nervous, because at that time, when I would feel the pain of others, in my dreams or as voices guiding me, I would become afraid. For this reason, I would only offer my gifts of healing when I felt safe. *Have no fear. Jesus is the way*, the guiding voice said as I walked out the door with Tillie.

The first thing I encountered when I arrived at the hospital, was how the nursing staff looked at me in a way I perceived as judgemental. Thankfully, I was able to ignore my feelings and focus on LeRae. I was committed to honouring the strong message I received in my dream in which I offered LeRae my healing gifts. I entered LeRae's room with Tillie. I placed my

---

[8] An aboriginal group of First Nations who inhabit the northern boreal and Arctic regions of Canada.

44

hands at the top of her head, while Tillie placed her hands on LeRae's feet. I closed my eyes and invoked a prayer in the name of Jesus. I prayed for LeRae to be able to communicate with her parents once again.

A spirit guide appeared and helped me pray for LeRae, as did a voice telling me about her condition and why she was hurting so much. This voice implied that she was extremely frustrated and that she was being held back because of the strain on her back. I knew, by this point, I could connect with her telepathically, and I set my intention through my thoughts. I encouraged her to be strong, not to worry, and that I felt she was going to be okay. As Tillie and I continued offering LeRae our healing gifts, LeRae's heart suddenly began to race.

Tillie

I remember while Alvin and I were working with LeRae, LeRae's heart rate elevated into the danger zone. I asked the nurses, who were in the room discussing LeRae's heart rate, "What is a normal heart rate?"

As soon as I asked the question, Alvin leaned over and said to LeRae, "You need to relax. There are people here who are helping you. You can do this. You just need to relax. Let us do our job. You just need to calm down and relax."

LeRae's heart rate started dropping, and I remember the nurse saying, "The meds must be working."

Alvin and I knew exactly what happened. LeRae had lowered her own heart rate the moment Alvin spoke to her. It was in that moment that I realized I could use the nurses to help me heal LeRae's pain by asking them about the morphine monitor that showed her pain level with bars. The bars showed LeRae was in great pain when I worked on her back. The moment I moved her bones back into place, the bars on the monitor completely disappeared. Again, the nurse who was watching the monitor couldn't believe what she saw and attributed it to the fact that the morphine was finally working and that it had nothing to do with what Alvin and I were doing. That's when Alvin leaned in and started talking to LeRae again. With his healing words, he led her to a safe place within her mind by telling her not to pay attention to what people were saying around her, that she was in charge, and it was up to her now to keep herself calm and relaxed. As he continued to help her regain her confidence, she ultimately learned how to calm herself down.

Alvin

I remember, when I was about four years old, I was the only person called to my grandmother's bedside before she passed. Because of her request, I was told I was special, that I was to be treated with respect, and that one day my skills would be needed. This was difficult for me to understand. As I became older, I was hard on myself and out of control at times, always wondering why I was chosen. Eventually, through my life experiences, I learned to accept things as they were, value my life, and appreciate the benefits of natural healing.

Visiting LeRae in the hospital was a humbling and life-changing experience. I knew I was there to help her. What I didn't know was how she was also meant to help me. The moment I placed my hands on her head, I instantly felt the prayers of all the people who were praying for her. It was an overwhelming feeling I had never felt before. I truly felt like I'd become an instrument of God and that Jesus was leading the way. My experience with LeRae also shifted my skepticism for my own healing abilities. She gave me the opportunity to trust in my skills, healing knowledge, and inner guidance more than I had before. It also opened me to the spiritual aspect of healing and to trusting my heart.

During one of my healing prayer offerings for LeRae, I was shown she would recover from this illness. I asked how long in my mind, and I received the number three—three days, three months, and three years. Three days later, after I shared this information with Tillie, LeRae was moving her head. In Jesus's name, I prayed.

∞

Tillie

Alvin shared the message he received during one of his prayer offerings for LeRae. I was encouraged. The following day, my client Rod arrived and told me he had a dream of LeRae. She was walking, but there was an issue with her big toe. This was confirmation for me. Beauty called the next day and LeRae was awake and communicating. I cried with relief. I cried with joy. My heart was no longer heavy. As soon as I was done with clients, I drove to hospital. This was a joyful day.

As anticipated, LeRae was months ahead of the expected recovery for someone with GBS. She defied the odds. I am forever grateful for Beauty's trust in me, thankful for my gifts, and honoured to have been a part of something so miraculous.

Six
The Blessing of Breath

Beauty

I became consciously aware of my breath at the age of thirty-three. During my spiritual awakening, I realized I was taking for granted the only thing giving me life. Until then, I didn't pay much attention to my breath or the significance of it. As I was healing, I learned that without my breath I would have no life and taking it for granted was no longer an option.

I learned how the lack or quality of my breath was directly connected to my pain and reconnecting to it was crucial to my recovery. This realization propelled me into a deep study of the breath, which led me to participate in numerous workshops, read an eclectic mix of books, and attend yoga classes that focused primarily on the breath. From there, I practiced an array of breathing techniques, each one connecting me to the resonance that my body, mind, and spirit needed to heal. I realized, then, that my whole body wanted to breathe—to expand and contract with the rhythm of the universe. Through a devoted practice, I taught myself how to consciously breathe, creating a stable foundation from which I began the process of healing. My first step was to focus on my breath, slow it down, and breathe deeply. I was fascinated to witness my physical body respond to this new way of breathing and how relaxed it became. As time passed, my devoted practice became second nature: it no longer felt like a practice—it became a way of life.

Witnessing LeRae, day after day, hooked up to a ventilating machine, was a profound experience. It awakened within me a deeper understanding of the blessing of breath. I didn't understand the magnitude of my experience or how it would play out in my life, until years later, when I was blessed with the opportunity to lovingly assist Tecla, who was like a mother to me, and my grandmother Marion into the light, each orchestrating their own unique divine passing until their last breath. This incredible honour reignited the commitment I made to myself after LeRae was taken off the ventilator: *For as long as I am breathing, I will give thanks for the blessing of my breath.*

Mystical Magical Miracle #8

Listening to music while LeRae was in PICU, or while I was driving to and from the hospital, was impossible. Each time I tried to turn on the radio, my body contracted, preventing me from pushing the button. Instead, I was guided to do three specific things to create a mantra: recite the Lord's Prayer, sing "Amazing Grace," and end with vocal toning. I chanted this powerful healing mantra for as many weeks as LeRae was on life support.

On November 16, 2006, during a cold, snowy, windy day, everything shifted. I was at home preparing for the drive back to the hospital when I noticed the weather had changed dramatically. The roads were icy, and the blizzard-like conditions had minimized visibility. To top it off, the sun was setting. I hopped into the van, backed out of the driveway, and began singing the healing mantra. The slow arduous drive back to the hospital created space for me to sing more rounds of the mantra. I was near the end of another round of vocal toning and about to recite the Lord's Prayer when I heard a deep harmonic tone coming from both outside and within me. The tone deepened and amplified, which made continuing my toning impossible. I suddenly became aware of what I was hearing. It was the Gregorian monks chanting the word *Aum*.[9]

The incessant, heavy feeling that was sitting on my chest lifted. Tears of gratitude poured down my face as the deep, primordial sound of Aum settled within my heart's centre. Loving words, layered with names, flowed in, first in English, then in foreign languages. I could no longer hear the word

---

[9] A Hindu chant/mantra meaning universal sound.

Aum or understand what I was hearing. Incredibly honoured, I tearfully said, "What is the message?"

> *This is The Universal Prayer of Life. Every loving thought and loving word spoken since the beginning of human existence is imbedded within this Universal Prayer. When you pray for one, you pray for all.*

"Holy mother of God," I cried out.

My understanding of this message was that every prayer, loving word spoken, and loving thought offered through a human being rests eternally within the sacred heart of divine love, floating freely within the mystical field of invisibility for all to access. When I pray for others, including myself, I am praying for all people.

The snow stopped falling, the wind settled, and I was about to drive, once again, across University Bridge. As I drove across the bridge, the names and words transformed into a beautiful musical composition, soothing my tender heart. By the time I parked my vehicle, The Universal Prayer had transcended into a unified harmonic sound, like the sound of a crystal singing bowl. It was loud, unshakable, and commanded my full attention as I entered LeRae's room.

"LeRae's lungs are strong enough. We'll be removing the ventilator tomorrow," the nurse said exuberantly.

"Yes!" I said, joyfully, as I jumped up and down with excitement. "I knew something amazing was going to happen. Thank you, thank you, thank you."

The sound of The Universal Prayer commanded my attention until November 30th, the day LeRae was transferred to room 3023 on the recovery unit. I was sitting on a lounge chair in the corner of the room watching LeRae sleep when a subtle wave of Zen-like energy flowed through me, preparing me for the divine message I was about to receive. Piercing through the soothing sound of The Universal Prayer, I heard, *It's time to listen to music again.* I knew I needed to listen to the CD my friend Jan had given to me. I put my earbuds in, closed my eyes, and pressed play.

"There I am," I tearfully whispered, as the angelic, ethereal voice of Deva Premal echoed through my entire body.

As the last song ended, The Universal Prayer faded into the depths of my awareness and became the undertone instead of the overtone. I was finally able to turn on the radio, listen to music, and write songs again.

November 17, 2006

Well, this has been an interesting day. The doctors told me they're removing the ventilator tomorrow, the only thing that's keeping me alive. Why did they have to tell me the day before? I don't feel ready. It's too early. Are my lungs strong enough? I need more time. What if I can't breathe on my own? They'll have to put it back in. No thank you!

Where's my shaker bottle, the one the nurses made for me to call for help? I'm not strong enough to use the call button. I'm scared and alone. There it is! Oh, shoot—it's too far away. Come on, just reach for it . . . Oh thank god, I have my fingers on it. If I could just grasp it . . . Oh my god—no! I just knocked it off the bed! Of all times for it to fall out of reach, why now—like really? Where is everyone? It feels like hours since anyone has checked on me. My heart is beating fast. I can feel my fear taking over. I need to calm down. I just want Mom, Dad, a nurse—anyone—to walk into my room. I need to see someone.

"She'll never walk again," "She still can't breathe on her own," "Her chance of a full recovery is minimal"—where are all these thoughts coming from? I feel terrified and confused. It's those silly doctors talking about me in front of me. Hello, even though I'm paralyzed and on life support, I can still hear you. I don't understand. Did they not read my chart?

I'm definitely going to die if I can't breathe on my own. Too many thoughts, too much going on in my mind. Even if I can breathe on my own, breathing will just be the beginning. I want to prove those doctors wrong—I want to walk again. How am I supposed to do that if I'm still paralyzed? What if my nerves don't regenerate? What if I fail? What if I can't do it? I want to walk again. I really, really, really want to walk again, to run, to dance, to be a teenager—I want my life back. I'm going to work harder than I ever have before. What if I can't? What if I'm paralyzed for life? Oh my god, these thoughts are driving me crazy! I

51

don't know how to break this cycle right now, not on my own. I need help. I need someone to come check on me already!

Finally, some people! Dad is rushing into the room with a nurse. Thank god. I need him. I need to feel safe. My heart is racing out of control and setting off all the machines. That's how they know something is wrong. I feel safe now. I feel like Dad can hear me, and he knows exactly how I feel. Even though I can't seem to shake these thoughts, I'm not alone, and that makes all the difference. Thank you for staying with me, tonight. Tomorrow is a big day for me, for all of us.

November 18, 2006

Okay, today is the day. I'm going to breathe on my own again. Holy crap. I have no choice. The machine is coming out, whether I like it or not. I'm so nervous. Last night was exhausting. I'm excited . . . sort of. The doctors think I can breathe on my own. I should trust them. Except, I'm terrified, because I don't know if I believe it. What if I'm not strong enough? What if I forget how? What if . . . Oh my god—shut up brain! You're being ridiculous and scaring the crap out of me.

This is a good thing. I can breathe on my own. No more nonsense about how I'm not strong or that I can't do it. I'm ready for this stupid thing to be out of me. I'm ready to breathe on my own. I can do this. I am strong.

The sun is shining on me. Dad says everything will be okay and that I'm able to breathe on my own. He says I don't need the ventilator anymore, and I believe him.

Well, here we go. They're all standing around me again. I wonder who'll be the lucky one with the privilege to take this thing out of me. Let's do this . . . Holy crap! This feels awful. The tube coming out of my throat is the most uncomfortable feeling. Good lord, it feels like there's a huge ribbed straw slicing up my throat. What the hell? I can feel every inch of it.

It's out! Oh my god, I'm hyperventilating. I can't stop. Help, somebody, please, help! Can I breathe? I can't tell. What the hell? I need help. Doctors and nurses are coaching me through. I can feel myself start to breathe normally. Sometimes I don't understand their ways, but I'm so thankful. I'm slowly gaining control over my breath. Every breath is a little bit deeper and a little bit longer.

Yes! It's gone. It's out of me. I'm breathing on my own, and I'm so proud of myself. I did it. I'm doing it! I'm breathing on my own, and I feel incredible. Wow, I forgot how amazing it feels to lay in bed without a ventilator. This feeling is almost indescribable. I feel warm, safe, and loved. I know I'm still in a hospital bed, but I feel completely different. I'm looking up at the lights. A peacefulness rushes over me, as I lay here listening to my breath. It's a foreign sound, compared to all the beeping I'm used to, it's beautiful.

I survived my battle of life and death. Now, I need to fight for the life I want to live. I need to fight for my legs, for my feet, and for my ability to walk.

On the plus side, I can talk again. Everyone is in for a real treat.

Seven
Metamorphoses

LeRae

November 21, 2006

Woah, that doesn't feel good! What the hell is going on now? Oh my god, my vagina hurts so much. Could it be a bladder infection? Or wait, maybe my nerves are firing up down there. That's a good thing. It's healing! Wow, it burns like crazy. Oh my god, no wonder—I still have a freaking catheter in! I need to pee, but the catheter is making it so uncomfortable. Mom talked to the nurse, and she said the catheter has to stay in, and I'm not allowed more pain medication for four hours. Four hours? Easy for her to say—she has no idea. It feels like hot coals are sitting on my vagina and ice-cold water is being poured on top. Lovely—wave after wave of burning pain. I think it's time to cry. Take some deep breathes and let the burning sensations pass. Okay, I can do this. I can wait. It's not that bad. It's only every few minutes. Oh god, that wave came much quicker than the last one! Oh no, please no, not again! I need this catheter out of me. I feel so helpless. I've been so strong and brave until now. I'm crumbling. Okay, just breathe. Just breathe. Thank God I can cry and for Mom, who is holding my hand as the burning sensations come and go.

My poor bladder. It's trying to figure out how the heck it's supposed to work with no help from the catheter. It's probably confused. Don't worry—so am I.

"Pee time," I say, with the strongest voice I can.

Saying it out loud is helping me. What is Mom doing?

"Mom, what are you doing?"

Hmmm, no answer. She's so focused. I can see a napkin, wrapped in plastic in her hands. Now it's over the catheter. I can feel the heat from her hands flowing into me. So comforting. What is she saying? It looks like she's reading something.

"What are you reading?" I ask through another wave of burning pain.

"I'm reciting the words on the back of this card. It's a prayer, called Medjugorje, written in Italian. Mother Mary is on the front, and it belongs with the napkin under my hands. Tecla gave it to me. She said it was blessed by the Pope, long ago. Close your eyes, sweetie. I need to continue."

I have no idea what she's saying, but I'm praying with her anyway. I'll do anything to make this pain go away. Mom has read that prayer like fifty times already. I can't keep up with her, I'm running out of prayers! I see the nurse. She's rushing into my room and with one yank my catheter is out. Well, if it was that easy, I would've done it myself. Tylenol, Thank God, or maybe I should thank Mother Mary. I can't believe it. It definitely hasn't been four hours. I'm so happy. Oh man, it feels good to have some control over my bladder. No more catheter means rehab is going to be in full force with Sergeant Travis leading the way. Now for my bowels to start working. I don't even want to think about that right now. Good lord.

Travis

I was touched and honoured that LeRae asked me to write a story about my experience as her physical therapist while treating her for GBS in 2006. My first thought was to write about how I felt as I moved through the process with her. My second thought was to write about the lessons I learned from LeRae. I didn't know how to put it all into words until I was sharing what I had learned with my colleagues and other patients who had been diagnosed with GBS. I realized, then, how much I continue to (anonymously) talk about my experience with her. I was also reminded of the amazing potential for recovery, even from severe cases. This was the reminder I needed to begin writing my story.

My first meeting with LeRae occurred shortly after she was admitted to PICU. She had already been intubated and ventilated for just under a week.

She was paralyzed from head to toe. She couldn't shake or nod her head, nor could she speak. The only voluntary muscle control she had was with her eyes. In the beginning, LeRae's parents lifted her eyelids, so she could communicate. Eyes up meant yes, and eyes down meant no. Eventually, she was able to blink twice for yes and once for no, which, for the family and healthcare workers, including myself, made figuring out what she needed a little easier.

One of our goals, while she was ventilated in PICU, was to maintain her range of motion, as much as possible. This was, in theory a simple job, considering her body was quite flaccid at the time. Many people with GBS suffer from hypersensitivity, especially to the hands and feet. Since LeRae's paralysis kept her from talking or grimacing, I sometimes wondered if I, by stretching her body was causing her extreme pain, mild discomfort, or just relaxing her. For me, it was a guessing game until the ventilator was removed a month later. After that, she could move her head, although she couldn't control it against gravity, and shrug her shoulders. I could also finally hear her voice! Finally, she was going to become an active participant in the rehab process.

She was quickly moved to the regular pediatric unit after the ventilator was removed. My first task with Jenn, the occupational therapist, was to mobilize her against gravity, something we had tried in PICU with limited success. I remember how, on the first day of sitting LeRae up, as I lowered her bed so her feet could be put on a stool, I suddenly heard a shrieking sound accompanied by a loud crunch from beneath the bed. I looked around the room, panicked and mystified, trying to figure out what had happened. I saw LeRae smirking while her mother, in disbelief, looked shocked. I didn't realize Beauty had placed a crystal healing stone under LeRae's bed until it seemed to shatter.

Beauty

I was guided to place a rose quartz crystal pyramid on the frame under LeRae's hospital bed, it was the only safe place to put it, where it wouldn't be swept away. The moment I heard the high-pitched screech and the shattering sound, I gasped out loud and put my hands over my mouth. Travis looked directly at me, eyes wide with a look of panic, as if to say, what the hell just happened? I thought for sure the crystal had shattered into thousands of pieces. I slowly reached under the bed and was pleasantly surprised. As I pulled the crystal out, I could see that only its tip had broken off and that the rest was amazingly still intact. I showed Travis the crystal, and he let out a big sigh of relief. Then we all, including LeRae, burst out laughing.

November 30, 2006

Can I lay down now? I'm really uncomfortable. Sitting up hurts like hell. Travis has my legs dangling off the bed, again. I didn't feel a thing when I was on the ventilator. Why is this so painful? So much pressure is surging through my entire body, pulling me down. I feel like my feet are attached to 150-pound weights.

"This exercise is meant to help increase the blood flow in your legs," Travis said, confidently

Well, buddy, if you don't lay me down soon, I'll increase the blood flow to your nose.

Thank goodness for Jenn. Her crazy curls and contagious smile are keeping me sane and willing to do Travis's intense rehab exercises. He talks a lot about a tilt table he wants me to try, soon. Pardon me? Sounds fun if I were at an amusement park, but in a hospital? No, thanks. I better be strapped in tight.

Oh, thank goodness—laying down feels good. Wow, my body feels more alive. The dangling must help bring life back into my body. I guess Travis really knows his stuff. I'll listen to him. He also knows when I'm being stubborn and understands my pain limits. I trust him. I just need to take this one day at a time. It will get easier, and I'll get better.

Shortly after the crystal incident, Jenn and I started using the tilt table as an alternative method of introducing LeRae's body to gravity. This was the first of many times when she became frustrated with me for pushing her beyond her comfort levels. The tilt table had three straps to block the knees, hips, and trunk. As soon as I thought she was able to handle an increased challenge, I would loosen the trunk strap with the table inclined. For someone with poor postural/trunk control, like LeRae, this was an extremely challenging activity. LeRae would repeatedly ask if we were done, and I repeatedly said, no. Even Jenn accused me of being a slave driver. While LeRae wasn't wrong, I don't regret pushing her outside her comfort zone, as this is a key part of therapy—the patient is supposed to be tired at the end of the treatment, and all activities should be achievable.

Each day, the activities steadily became more difficult for LeRae and were extended over longer periods. It was clear to me that LeRae was making gains, albeit slowly. This made perfect sense, since she was suffering from a severe case of GBS. Initially, when LeRae was assessed in the rehab program at City Hospital, she was declined, because she was unable to tolerate the amount of time necessary to complete the program—an excess of four hours a day, which included tolerating sitting in a wheelchair for at least two hours at a time. This was when Jenn and I decided to dedicate as much time as possible to building LeRae's strength and endurance, so we could achieve these requirements.

Typically, Jenn and I see patients in twenty-to thirty-minute blocks during the day. To help LeRae, we began offering her at least an hour a day. Given her steady gains, high desire to improve, and participation, justifying the time and resources for her extra therapy was easy. She was in the physio gym every day, working on transfers, core control, and cardiovascular fitness. Ongoing issues with pain, especially in her hands and feet, limited how much we were able to progress with standing activities. We were able to do functional activities: sitting, kneeling, and crawling (once her hands started to improve). Her feet were extremely hypersensitive, which was why it took so long for her to handle the pressure of her own body weight.

LeRae

December 3, 2006

    Travis and Jenn want me to try to stand with the horizontal bars in the physio gym today. I'll have to hold my entire body weight all by myself. I don't weigh much anymore—I'm skin and bones—so how bad could it be?

    My heart is pounding. Travis is positioning my wheelchair in between the bars and now is standing in front of me. I'm supposed to do what? Pull myself up? I haven't done that in over a month. Jenn is behind me, holding onto the transfer belt around my waist. I need her because I won't be able to pull myself up on my own. Well, here goes nothing. One, two, three . . . holy crap! My hands, my hands! It hurts. There's so much pressure. I can't feel my legs. All I feel is a numbing, tingling sensation pulsing through my hands. I feel like I'm going to pass out. I don't think I can do this for much longer. I need help.

    "Help, I don't want to fall to the floor," I blurt out.

    My dream team comes to the rescue. Thank goodness, I'm safely back in my chair.

    "How long was I standing?" I asked.

    "Ten seconds," Travis said.

    "Seriously?" I asked, gasping.

    What? Are you being honest? That's it? It felt like hours! Who knew going through hellfire pain could feel so satisfying. Standing on my own two feet for only ten seconds felt exhilarating and exhausting. I don't know why, but I'm excited to do it again tomorrow. I hope you two know what you're getting yourselves into!

December 4, 2006

    What in the world? It feels like there are thousands of tiny needles stabbing into my toes. Oh my god, is the GBS coming back?

    "Mom, wake up. Wake up—my toes feel like they're on fire!" I said in a panic.

    "You're okay. You're okay. It isn't the GBS coming back. Your toes are starting to heal, and your nerves are regenerating."

    "Can I have more nerve medication?" I pleaded.

    "No sweetie, you're topped up for tonight."

    Come on. This pain is way too intense. This isn't fair.

"I have an idea," Mom says.

"Okay, what is it?" I said, desperately.

And there she goes, running out of the room again. Well, that was quick. She's carrying ice packs and warm blankets. This could be interesting. She's trying as hard as she can to ease my pain by switching the ice packs with warm blankets. Wow, it's working! What an amazing mother! I think I'm falling asleep.

"Oh, my toes, my toes! Mom, they feel like they're on fire, again. Can I have some medication now?"

She grabs the ice packs and puts them on my toes.

"No! It's too much. I can't handle it," I tearfully said.

"Okay, my love. This is one of those times when I'm unable to help you manage the pain. This one's up to you. I know the pain is unbearable, so you need to use the power of your mind, just like you've been doing all along. Focus on something other than the pain. Go to that peaceful place you've already created in your mind."

"You're so good to me," I said, gratefully, and closed my eyes.

My whole body sighs. Surrendering to the pain, I feel a wave of peace wash over me. I stop focusing on the pain. I can feel myself expand and my entire body fill with empty space. I'm floating. I feel safe. The pain is still here, but I'm not affected by it anymore. My mind is filled with a vast emptiness and the pain is only a tiny speck. I'll rest here for now.

December 11, 2006

What's that noise? I'm trying to sleep! Of course, go figure. I'm finally having a good sleep and who shows up? The one, the only, Travis. Don't you know by now I'm not a morning person? The nurses gave me an extra sleeping pill last night, so this physio session should be interesting. He wants to do more core exercises today. Good luck.

Oh my god, I can't stop laughing. I haven't giggled this much in so long. Everything is funny. Travis and Jenn have me on my hands and knees, and I'm giggling out of control. I'm so out of it. What in the world is in those sleeping pills? Travis is not impressed. It's all work and no play with him in the physio gym. I guess my giggling is contagious, because Jenn can't stop laughing either. This is great, and the look on Travis's face is priceless. Okay, I need to be serious. Yeah, right!

Travis has had enough. I know he wants me to get better as fast as I can. He's not thrilled about this session. He tells me to slide over and sit on the large bosu ball. Smart move, Travis. He knows I'll have to concentrate or roll right off.

"Catch!" *Travis says, as he threw a medicine ball at me.*

"Whoa, man!" *I say, giggling.* "This thing is heavy."

What's with that look on your face, Travis? Did you think I wasn't going to catch it? Wait a minute, I did catch it, and I'm still balancing on the bosu ball. My core is getting stronger! Yahoo!

"Catch!" *I laugh as I throw it back to Travis.*

Finally, a smile. Oh, look, there's my parents.

Travis

Another memorable day was when LeRae came down to see Jenn and I without her parents. We were happy with her progress with the wheelchair and were eager to try a new activity with her—sitting on a therapy ball. This activity requires a great deal of core stability. It was a particularly challenging day for LeRae; however, Jenn and I were impressed with what she was able to achieve. Towards the end of the session, her parents arrived, and we thought LeRae would have been excited to tell them what she had achieved. We excitedly suggested that she tell them what we were doing. Much to our surprise, LeRae yelled out, at the top of her voice to her parents across the gym, "They've been trying to kill me!" Little did she know, she had reached her goal, and shortly after that session, LeRae was transferred to rehab at City Hospital two and a half months after being admitted to Royal University Hospital.

LeRae made an incredible impact on my life. She achieved in a short time what was, at times, considered a long shot. I keenly remember speaking with a fellow colleague who, several months after she was discharged from rehab, said they had seen LeRae at the gym briskly walking on the treadmill. She truly is a remarkable young woman who fought back against a terrible situation and made an incredible recovery.

Jennifer

I was new to pediatrics at Royal University Hospital when I learned of a teenage girl named LeRae transferred to PICU. I was informed she was dealing with Guillain-Barré and would need to remain in PICU for some time. As soon as LeRae was stable, she was transferred back to Pediatrics 3000 to continue her road to recovery.

Hesitantly, I approached LeRae and her parents, unsure how they would react to a recreation therapist being involved at this time. Without hesitation, LeRae and her parents accepted my invitation to explore her past and present leisure lifestyle choices, along with adaptations and new interests.

LeRae's initial recovery was slow. Before her diagnosis, LeRae was a healthy, independent, active, and athletic young woman. She loved going out with her friends, dancing, doing gymnastics, and talking about boys. Her prognosis of a full recovery, was slim. When she arrived back at Pediatrics 3000, she was confined to her bed, and her body had to relearn everything. Mom and Dad were always there to help. Dad was inviting, with a soft personality and a big heart. I often watched him proudly take care of LeRae's needs. Mom was out-going, easy to talk to, down to earth, protective, and open to all who were there to assist with LeRae's recovery. I thought how lucky I was to be a part of this family's journey.

LeRae and I came to know each other through visits and talks. She was quiet and inviting. At the beginning, LeRae listened as I shared many stories. Slowly, she began to share more about who she was and what she liked. It was apparent what a wonderful young woman LeRae was. She worked hard every day with physiotherapy, occupational therapy, and me. We had to schedule around family time, naps, self-care, and visits with friends. In our discussions, LeRae stated she wasn't crafty but, because of her current condition, she wanted to challenge herself by painting—she'd chosen to paint a wooden box. During each scheduled visit, LeRae painted what she could, progressing from an edge, to a smaller side, a larger top, and continuing, ordering her hands to work, while huffing and puffing along the way. Within a week, with many UNO games mixed in, which she almost always won, she finished her box. She'd painted it with many colours, and it was as beautiful as her. I was incredibly proud. You would think that something like this wouldn't be so hard, but, when all your muscles, big and small, are learning how to work again, anything beyond just sitting still is exhausting.

LeRae was a calm fighter. She wasn't afraid to work hard, break some sweat, and tell those muscles, out loud, what to do. Through it all, she never complained. She only wanted to move forward a little more each day. Her mom was always near by, watching LeRae closely, while taking care of her own mind, body, and soul through holistic healing/teaching. She believed in a holistic, healthy lifestyle, which included what goes into the body. I always laughed when I would walk in and LeRae was fiercely fighting with her hands to feed herself a Dairy Queen Blizzard, something she asked for daily. Beauty would shake her head and smile from ear to ear, telling me later how she was mixing a product called NuPlus into LeRae's Blizzards for nutritional support.

LeRae's stubbornness, independence, and drive took her far in her recovery. Her smile was contagious. I never left her room feeling down or sorry for her, and she never wanted pity either. She expected to be treated like the young woman she was, with no special treatment, allowing others to help when she was unable to do it herself. As LeRae continued to progress, the time finally came for her to be transferred to City Hospital for more intensive rehabilitation. She said her goodbyes, and off she went, ready for the next stage. I knew she would do well. I didn't know how well until one day, there she was, walking towards me, independently, and smiling that big, beautiful smile. She had come back to pediatrics to say hello to everyone. All I could do was cry and hug her.

To this day, that memory makes me smile and cry. I am so proud of LeRae's accomplishments. LeRae and her family reminded me of what is possible when you work together, believe in each other, love one another, and open your lives to all the support around you.

Eight
Immaculate Magnificent Love

Beauty

The moment LeRae was ventilated, an indescribable force, far beyond anything my mind could conceive or my heart contain, ignited within me. I'd never experienced this feeling before. It rose up from my unbearable grief and transformed into an overpowering, profound feeling that urged me to act. From the shadowlands of my despair, this feeling transformed into an unstoppable, lifesaving force. It embodied the grace of a swan, the patience of a butterfly, and the peace of a dove. It also embodied an unimaginable fury of luminous light, transcending and transmuting all that was dark into benevolent love with the words "Thy will be done" echoing in the background.

I was humbled to my knees, many times, in awe and wonder of how immaculate and magnificent this loving force can be. At one point, sobbing into my hands, I cried, "Oh my God, we are all loved this much. LeRae is loved this much. I am loved this much."

The letters and stories you are about to read were written by LeRae's family and friends—people who love her dearly and who offered their own unique, immaculate, magnificent love to save her. Walking into her room in PICU was like walking into a rainbow. I could see and feel all the colours and multidimensional layers of love hovering above her. I witnessed this love overflow into the rooms around her, healing all those who were near. It was one of the most beautiful things I've ever seen.

Nana Carol

LeRae, as I sit here, trying to put my thoughts in print about your journey, tears are streaming down my face. This is what happens every time I remember the first two months you were in the hospital, fighting to recover from a serious bout of GBS. The first time I saw you in PICU at Royal University Hospital was devastating. I knew my grief would not help you, and it took everything I had to keep it together. Over the course of the month you were on life support, I spent many hours at your bedside, holding your hand, reading to you, and keeping you company. I visited the chapel often. I truly believed that with your determined nature you would overcome the poor prognosis given to you by some doctors. I also believed you would be a survivor, no matter how long it took, and you are!

You had many ups and downs during your three-month stay in the hospital, and you were a constant inspiration to me. It was rewarding for me to play "taxi driver" for some of your visiting school friends, who kept you "in the loop."

January 3rd was a hallelujah day. You were discharged from the hospital and home to stay. I was overjoyed and thankful that the family unit was together again. During the tough times, I had my faith to sustain me and the support of family and friends, many of whom still inquire about your health. When I look at you today, leading a full and active life, I feel truly blessed and incredibly grateful I can still share your awesome hugs.

Papa Ken

On October 18, 2006, Carol and I were visiting my brother and his wife in Ontario. We were returning to their home after sightseeing when I experienced an uneasy feeling that someone was trying to get an important message to me. I asked my brother if he had checked the answering machine, and he said, no. This was the first thing I did when we arrived back at their home. There was a message from Ed to call as soon as possible. I then learned the devastating news that LeRae was in intensive care and seriously ill. Within an hour, Carol and I packed up and started the drive home.

The trip back was a blur, and I have no recollection of any conversation. I do remember crossing the border at Sarnia without any problem (a first) and the weather being cold and rainy. We arrived in Saskatoon, late afternoon, on October 22, and drove directly to the hospital. The news wasn't good. I learned that the medical team, because LeRae's condition was so rare, was in touch and discussing LeRae's treatment with other physicians all over North America. Mom or Dad or both were by her side 24/7 and had been doing that since she was admitted. I was informed by Ed of the sequence of events leading to the stage she was in, and I was worried. I was also mad and upset because I didn't know what was happening to her or why. I tried to tell myself she is strong and everything will be fine, but there she was, laying paralyzed from the neck down and hooked up to the ventilating machine. Her team was discussing a couple of possibilities about how to proceed with her treatment—the wrong treatment could be harmful.

I became angry. Why couldn't they find the answer? I think the doctor finally decided on a treatment simply because something had to be done quickly. His diagnosis pointed to GBS. I decided to research what GBS was on the internet, and what I read was terrible. Most people survive; however, LeRae had the fourth stage. Even if she survived, she would be left with lasting side effects.

I recall the day I walked past Ed and Beauty's patio door and noticed a flickering light on the table. I entered. On the table was a lit candle, a picture of LeRae, some flowers, other things she loved, and gifts from other people. I knew these were for hope and life. It was an overpowering, memorable moment I will always remember.

I desperately needed to help LeRae. I knew she was strong, mentally and physically, and that she had lots of will power before she became ill. However, at the stage she was in, I felt a reserve would be good. I proceeded to have a one-sided conversation while sitting by her bedside and told her to take my reserve.

I remember the pain she had to endure as she was improving, and how it was alleviated, when Doriana, a nurse, came to visit. Doriana immediately asked the hospital staff to put in a PIC line and to keep the blanket's weight off her feet. This, I feel, helped LeRae considerably in her recovery. With her sheer will power and determination, she beat up on GBS and kicked its ass to the curb. Through extensive rehab and hard work, she returned her frail, ravaged body back to its original shape and began accomplishing things she was told she would never do again. I am so proud of her.

Uncle Curtis

(Aunt Tami & Zach)

I don't remember very much from that time. What I do remember is we were not prepared for anything like GBS or how serious it is. We found out LeRae had GBS on a Saturday morning in October 2006, when my wife Tami, my son Zach, and I were planning a regular outing to the mall. I had just finished my coffee and was goofing around on my guitar when the phone rang. What began as a regular day of shopping turned into a down day. I recall being told LeRae was on a ventilator and that she could no longer move or speak, but that she could still hear.

It was hard to believe this was happening, and no one was sure what lay ahead. Faith, hope, and healing were front and centre. We just didn't know how it would play out. As the weeks progressed, LeRae made limited improvement. However, by November and December, the news was more uplifting. She was gradually regaining movement and progressing. By Christmas, LeRae was home for the holidays. This was simply amazing.

I wrote the following words shortly after LeRae came home from the hospital: "Life is precious. All the things you want to do and achieve are worth chasing. Each person needs to make the most of it and appreciate everything around them. Be grateful, show respect, and make sure to give back." (Both my wife, Tami, and I still feel this way today.)

LeRae faced adversity that our family wasn't prepared for. Thankfully, LeRae mustered the courage to get through it. That, to us, is enough to keep believing in the will of the human spirit!

Grandma Helen

I felt devastated, worried, and scared when I heard the news about LeRae. When I visited her for the first time, she was laying there, paralyzed from the neck down. I didn't know what to do or what to think. It was terrible. She had every kind of tube necessary to keep her alive. I have a vivid memory of when the ventilator was going to be taken out.

The doctors decided to tell her the night before. This bothered me because Ed said she couldn't sleep all night. I think they should have waited and told her in the morning to keep her from becoming so worried. Thankfully, Ed stayed with her all night and helped her stay calm.

Another vivid memory I have is of when LeRae was moved from PICU to the observation room—even though she was doing better, she had a long way to go. I also remember the evening when she was extremely constipated. We were all trying our best to console her, when she suddenly blurted out, "If this is what it's like to have a baby, I don't want one!" Everyone chuckled. Even in her dire circumstance, she could get a chuckle out of people and still does.

LeRae's illness was hard on everybody, especially her brother Austin. He didn't know how his sister was doing and whether she was going to live. My heart went out to him, as well.

LeRae has come a long way and has worked hard in her recovery. Thankfully, everything worked out for the best!

Aunt Judy

I entered LeRae's room feeling positive and hopeful while offering my support through prayer. I remember whispering healing words into her ear, when suddenly her shoulders began moving up and down. She had been unable to do this until I whispered in her ear. Seeing her move like this was a joyful and amazing experience, and I felt she knew me.

I didn't know what GBS was or how devastating it could be before LeRae became ill. Thankfully, she is a survivor. She and her family always had hope. Never lose hope.

Beauty

Aunt Judy was standing on the left side of LeRae's hospital bed, conversing with my mom. Unexpectedly, she leaned in and whispered something into LeRae's ear. Seconds later, LeRae's head and shoulders moved up and down.

"Oh my God," I shouted, "She just shrugged her shoulders. What did you say to her?"

"A prayer," she responded, as my mom followed with an exuberant, "Halleluiah."

I believe the moment Aunt Judy spoke into LeRae's ear was the same moment Scott's long-distance healing gift synchronized with her prayer. This was another amazing experience of witnessing the miraculous healing power of prayer and intention. My father summed up the hero's of LeRae's journey beautifully. He wrote:

> "My heroes the hundreds of people who prayed and sent messages that made her room bright and full of hope.
>
> Special heroes: my business associates, especially the moms who ran the order desks, who offered me great support, and with whom, for over forty years, I could share my concerns. Three were already familiar with GBS and were genuinely concerned about LeRae's wellbeing. To this day, they still ask me how my granddaughter is doing, and I say, "Just fine. Thank you." A business associate, whom I consider a friend, shared his story about having GBS while LeRae was in recovery. He is a tall, strong, athletic man, but still,

at the time, had side effects from the GBS. I asked him if he would visit LeRae in the hospital while she was in recovery, to reinforce the fact that she would get better. He didn't hesitate, and I will be forever thankful.

Super heroes: my wife Carol, G.G. (my mother-in-law), grandmothers, aunts, LeRae's friends, doctors, nurses, all LeRae's caregivers, and the physiotherapy team.

Big Super heroes: LeRae's mom and dad. They didn't eat or sleep properly for months. I could see this beginning to show on their bodies, and I'm sure it affected them mentally as well. I wasn't happy seeing this happening to them, yet they had no choice. Only after a long time did I notice a positive change in their physical appearance. Mentally, though, they were strong and seemed to be doing well, especially when LeRae came home from the hospital."

LeRae was moved from the observation unit to the recovery unit, no longer needing round-the-clock care from the nursing staff. I had become one of LeRae's primary caregivers, while she was in PICU. This made my transition into the recovery unit as her "private nurse" effortless. My training, as a medical office assistant helped me do this. In the beginning, the nursing staff watched my every move, and, after observing me with LeRae, they could clearly see I knew what I was doing. Of course, they continued to check her vital signs, administer her medication, and make sure she was comfortable. I was able to help LeRae with everything else. When I was unavailable, Ed and my mom stepped in. At one point, they both needed to step in longer than I wanted to them to.

After LeRae was moved from PICU to the observation unit Ed and I were able to, individually, stay entire nights with her. We decided that staying two nights in a row, then switching, would work best for us. We made sure LeRae was never alone by having other family members sit with her until one of us arrived. This worked beautifully until I decided I could handle staying three nights in a row. I was on the fourth night when one of the doctors, matter-of-factly, asked to talk to me outside.

"When you stay the night, do you sleep?" she asked, and proceeded to stand directly in front of me.

"No, I drift in and out of sleep because LeRae always needs something during the night."

"I've been watching you closely, and you're unaware that you're becoming delirious. I'm sending you home with a prescription for two mild sleeping pills, and I want you to take them as soon as you get there."

"No, that's okay. I'm fine. I can handle it," I said confidently.

She took a deep breath, looked down, and gently wrapped her hands around mine. She slowly lifted her head and looked deep into my eyes.

"No, you're not," she said firmly. "Please, you must go home, doctor's orders."

I felt something shift inside of me. I realized she was right. She reached into her pocket, pulled out a pad of paper, and wrote out a prescription for two sleeping pills.

"This is all you need," she said lovingly.

I walked back into LeRae's room and told everyone I was going home.

"You need to take care of yourself now, mommy," LeRae said happily with a big smile on her face.

She is right, I thought. I walked out the door, with tears rolling down my face.

I was sitting on a chair, in our living room, contemplating whether I should swallow the two pills or just continue holding them. I was hesitant. I didn't want to miss anything. I heard a knock from next door and, before I could say come in, my father entered. We live together in our family home, which was renovated into a unique duplex. My parents' bedroom door opens into our living room. My father slowly opened the door and took two steps forward. Before he could take his next step, I burst into tears, jumped out of my chair, and threw myself into his arms, hugging him tightly. He held me in silence, until I stopped crying. In those few precious moments, I was able to release my fear of taking the sleeping pills and to vocalize my dilemma.

"Everything will be okay. I promise she'll be taken care of. You need to take the pills," he said, with conviction.

He gently sat me back down in the chair, brought me a glass of water and waited until I swallowed the two pills. He watched me walk to the bedroom, where I proceeded to sleep for twelve hours. I woke up feeling completely re-energized and like a new person. The best part was walking back into LeRae's room and seeing her with one of her friends. She was beaming with joy. As I reached in to give her a hug, my father's words came rushing in: *Everything will be okay. I promise, she'll be well taken care of.* And she was.

Crystal

LeRae and I were best friends in high school. When I received the phone call, I thought, oh my god, this can't be happening. That night was an emotional night for both me and my father, because LeRae was also close to him. My first few visits to PICU, at Royal University Hospital, were difficult. I was trying to keep it together and stay strong. I remember leaving the room after each visit with tears streaming down my face and sadness in my heart. Thankfully, her wonderful parents were there to support me, by giving me a shoulder to cry on and someone to talk to. Eventually, my visits became easier.

School wasn't the same without LeRae. I missed her skipping down the halls and greeting me with hugs and complements. To try and lift her spirits, LeRae's friends and I, made her cards and posters which I took to the hospital, where I read them out loud to her. I remember during one of my initial evening visits, I didn't know what to say to her, so I just spoke to her through my mind, not thinking she would receive my messages. I was telling her to stay strong and fight as hard as she could to get better and that I loved her dearly. To my surprise, the next morning, when I woke up, I felt this overwhelming, strong vibe that she was talking back to me through her thoughts. I was so pleased that I started crying again—happy tears this time, because I knew she was going to be alright.

My visits to the hospital became easier. I started talking about my day, what new songs I'd heard, a new boy I liked, and stuff about my life I knew she wouldn't want to miss out on. I continued to try to keep her spirits up by keeping her updated and telling her how much I missed her. I felt like it was working.

My heart lit up when she was finally able to open her eyes. From that moment, every time I would visit LeRae, she was better. I was able to make her smile and laugh again, which was the best feeling ever for me. Before I knew it, LeRae was going home. I remember the day she came back to school in a wheelchair. For me, things seemed like they were back to normal. After school, I would visit her at home, almost every day, hanging out and talking about everything we could think of. My friendship with her felt stronger than ever, and I was more than happy to support her when she started to walk again. Her healing progressed faster than I would ever have imagined. She regained her strength and ability to do almost everything she had done before and more.

I am thankful for the opportunity to have been a part of her incredible journey. She has grown into a strong healthy independent woman, and no one would ever know that anything like that happened to her.

Keejara

I clearly remember the day I visited LeRae for the first time in the hospital. It was after the weekend was over, and I had many things to tell her. They were typical teenage girl things and, since we shared everything with each other, I couldn't wait to tell her. That day was hard! I walked into the room, and LeRae was laying in her hospital bed. She had one eye slightly open. When she looked at me, I could tell she wanted to speak to me, although this was impossible because of the ventilator. I remember feeling awkward, and I wanted to talk, but I was hesitant, because there were nurses in the room. I just started telling her about my weekend anyway, and I felt better. I told her about the drama, the gossip, and the current boy I had a crush on. All the normal things she was missing out on that I wished she was there for.

She and I were attached at the hip. I remember fighting back tears, while having a one-sided conversation with her, trying to act like everything was okay. I didn't want her to feel sad, and I wished it didn't have to be this way. I wished she could respond to me, laugh with me, and I wondered if she could even hear me. I also wondered why this had to happen to such a good friend.

Going through this with her was hard for me, but harder for her. She was unbelievably strong through it all. I am lucky to say LeRae and I are still friends.

Nine
Answering the Call

Beauty

We can all heal ourselves. We must each remember this truth, so we can reclaim our sovereignty, empower ourselves, and teach others along the way. Through my awakening journey, I've learned a valuable teaching: when someone has fallen, someone has risen. The strength of the person who has risen can hold the hand of the one who has fallen and lift them back into their own light.

LeRae began sending an SOS the moment she was placed in the ambulance. I can still hear her soulful plea—*I want to live. I want to live*—which she sent to whoever was open and willing to hear her.

Kahmaria

In the name of Our Father, Our Almighty Creator, I pray that You will lay Your powerful healing hands on LeRae Faulkner right now. I faithfully ask that at this very instant, You will send Your Holy Spirit to comfort her and her family and give them all the strength they need to overcome this battle. I pray that You will guide the knowledge and skills of her doctors right now and that Beauty and her family will feel Your Holy Presence as they stay by LeRae's side. In Jesus' name I pray and give You thanks for what You've already done and what You plan to do. Amen. (2006)

Jan

she couldn't breathe, at least, not on her own
yet my daughter's heart was beating in time with hers
and tied to every breath she didn't take
I truly believe in the power of prayer,
somehow, it just didn't seem to be
well, enough
it was in the wake of that not-enoughness
that I learned the power of dedication
we were in the basement of The Refinery
all assembled in our given roles
me in the 'teacher's' seat,
yogi's meticulously lined up on their magic carpets
all of us
awaiting guidance
in the space between words
where truth and magic reside
it came
'dedicate the breath to LeRae
ask them to breathe for her'
and so I did
and they did
and magic happened,
and the essence of the One True Heart (dare I say 'My Heart')
that beats in perfect time with the Mother of us all
slipped out of my soul as silent tears
gently carved a lineage of love
down the skin of my face

Beauty

Heavenly Sisters

I met the first heavenly sister, one of LeRae's nurses, when LeRae was admitted to PICU at Royal University Hospital, and I instantly felt safe and loved. She proceeded to effortlessly treat my family like we were her family and LeRae her daughter. Her vibrant personality, compassionate heart and ability to remain steady were a few of the angelic traits that I witnessed as she cared for LeRae. She was also fiercely devoted to her faith and belief in the power of prayer.

"Is it alright if I pray over LeRae?" she asked one morning, just before her shift was about to begin.

I gave her a big hug. "I'm okay with it, but I need to ask LeRae first."

I walked over to LeRae, lifted both her eyelids and asked if the nurse could pray over her. LeRae's eyes shot up like rockets, meaning a big yes. From that moment, this heavenly nurse prayed over LeRae and for our family non-stop. As time passed, she asked if her sister could come to the hospital and join her in prayer as well. The answer was another resounding yes. Together, they prayed over LeRae until she was transferred to City Hospital. Each time they offered a prayer, I felt the energy of their sacred words radiate from deep within their hearts. Bathed in their infinite belief in the power of prayer, I witnessed an abundance of spontaneous healings. Some were visible; others were a simple knowing. I'm deeply grateful for the extra care, love, and compassion these two heavenly sisters unconditionally offered LeRae and our family.

I'm also deeply grateful to Reverend M. McKechney for gathering our family together to facilitate a prayer circle for LeRae in the Royal University Hospital chapel. She guided us in prayer, then asked each of us to imagine we were breathing for LeRae. This was a powerful and unforgettable experience.

I was shown, how an extraordinary, magnificent, omnipotent power is activated when three or more people gather in a circle for the highest good of another. This is what I call a circle of grace and is what happened for LeRae. People from all over the world, from all walks of life, gathered together to offer their love, faith, and belief in something greater than themselves, creating an invisible unified field of grace where miracles happen. It was the moment I fully understood the miraculous healing power of prayer and the belief in the one called God, Goddess, Great Spirit, Yahweh, Source, Creator, Universe, and so on.

Brenda

It all started for me in my classroom near the end of a school day. My sister Debbie, who is close friends with LeRae's family, phoned me on my cell phone. Normally, my cellphone is turned off during class, but this time I had left the ringer on. I joked with my students that I needed to stop class to answer it, because it was probably from God (we all chuckled a bit at that). When I answered and found out it was my sister with a serious prayer request for a girl named LeRae and her family, I stopped joking. I acknowledged that I believed God had allowed the phone call to come through, so we could pray for LeRae right away. I relayed what little information I had learned about her quickly progressing condition to my students, and we all prayed. A short time after, I went to other classrooms full of students and asked them to join us in prayer as well. For the next few days, as we prayed, the students conveyed that they wished to do more than just pray. They were unsure what would be appropriate, so we made a card, a little video, and added a large stuffed animal. My husband Jos and I drove to Saskatoon with the little token gifts my students had prepared, unsure what we would do when we arrived except pray.

A couple of unusual things happened on our trip. First, Jos developed a cold sore on his lip, something he'd never had before and found annoying. When we arrived in Saskatoon, my sister Deb arranged with LeRae's grandma (Carol) to drop off the items at the hospital. I was also informed we wouldn't be able to visit LeRae or Beauty in PICU; however, we were welcome to stop in the hospital chapel to pray. When we arrived, Carol asked if Jos would remain in the lobby and not go up to the chapel until we returned. We didn't know why she asked that, but Jos was fine with it. While we went up to pray, Carol again confirmed we still wouldn't be able to chat with LeRae or Beauty.

Meanwhile, Jos explained to me, later, how he'd decided to read the newspaper at a table in the lobby. After reading for a bit, he felt compelled to go to the hospital pharmacy to buy medication for his cold sore. Just as he was getting up to leave, he had a strange feeling that he should leave his newspaper on the table (he remembers this clearly) and followed his instincts. No sooner had he left the area, Beauty walked passed his table and noticed the newspaper. Something also compelled her to stop at that table and look at the paper, because, when my sister Deb and I stepped out of the elevator, Beauty was sitting where Jos had been. Deb brought me over to her right away and introduced me. After chatting, Deb left, leaving the two of us to talk. By the time we were done talking, we'd both agreed that our meeting was a God-inspired moment and that we were perfectly set up to meet and talk.

I believe our connection was a clear sign God was confirming that Beauty, LeRae, and her whole family were visible to Him. Many things seemed to be going on, of which we were only a small part. After returning to Winnipeg, my students and I continued to lift the family up in prayer until the end of the school year. For us, this was a year when we were able to pray for several people in hard situations and, in this, see God's work. God was doing the miraculous, and we feel blessed to have been able to pray, watch, and rejoice in the healing of others.

Doriana

I have known LeRae her whole life. My experience with her and GBS is a bit different than others'. I am a nurse who works in an intensive care unit and have taken care of people who have suffered from GBS. When I found out LeRae's diagnosis, I knew her journey was going to be long and hard. I also knew I would be able to support LeRae and her family by offering my knowledge, not only about the treatments and machines needed for her recovery, but, more importantly, about what was happening to her. GBS has no cure. The treatments support the body and allow the illness to run its course.

Visiting LeRae in PICU didn't bother me, as this environment is my comfort zone—I can easily ignore the machines and all the beeps and noises. I was able to see LeRae as a normal, fifteen-year-old teenage girl and focus on her psychological care, instead of on the GBS. Once she was transferred to pediatrics, I was able to visit her often. I always brought the most current magazines, so we could critique what the movie stars were wearing and keep up to date on the entertainment gossip. We even planned how we would fly to Italy to crash Tom Cruise and Katie Holmes's wedding. I knew this was a fun distraction for her that would also help keep her mind off the GBS. Too often, I have witnessed patients become lost in their illness while in the ICU environment.

I remember asking LeRae what she really wanted to eat. "A chocolate shake and cheezies," she exuberantly said. After that, each time I would visit her, I brought a chocolate shake and some cheezies. Beauty would shake her head and smile, because she knew these foods had no nutritional value, as did I, but for a teenage girl recovering from a life-threatening illness, I felt they were a fun way to bring normalcy to a dire situation.

LeRae's journey with GBS taught me many valuable lessons. For me, LeRae's circumstance was more about attitude and spirit than the GBS. In all the times I visited her, I never once saw LeRae let the illness bring her down. I believe it was her positive attitude and sheer determination that helped her overcome this illness in a shorter time. The patients I have cared for in the past who had GBS often remained on life support for months. For LeRae to be out of the PICU in a month was remarkable. I believe being young and healthy, along with having a positive and determined attitude, contributed to LeRae's speedy recovery. She never let anything stop her. For example, when she arrived at the pediatrics unit, she wanted to connect with her friends from school. The only way for her to do this was to message them on the computer using MSN. This was challenging for her, because she barely had use of her hands. She would take minutes to type a simple word like *hello* and at least an hour to have a conversation. She was able to push through the pain and communicate with her friends, which ultimately played an essential role in her recovery.

Many factors contributed to LeRae's speedy recovery. I believe two of them were her positive attitude and her shining spirit. Both factors enabled her to overcome the challenges of GBS and are also the qualities that made her into the beautiful young lady she is today. I am truly proud of you LeRae.

Leanne

An evening of music, song, and creativity. Two women—they danced together that night. I was moved. So brave, beautiful, and vulnerable they seemed in their generational exchange and gender synchronicity.

I recall learning of the older woman, Beauty, my age, through a mutual friend and music-related connections. I was attending a workshop. We sat near each other and felt each other's kindred spirit. We began to talk and quickly realized who the other was.

A short time later, I heard that the younger woman, LeRae, was in the hospital with some unexplainable health crisis, an unknown infection or virus that was very serious.

Through email, I contacted Beauty, my new friend and kindred spirit. I wanted her to know I was caring for her and her family and that I was sending healing energy and love.

My life carried on—full of family, work, music, peace, and creative activities. From time to time, my friend, her daughter, and her family would come to my mind and heart, and I would then send warm energy or a thinking-of-you email.

Then a dream—half awake, half asleep, I felt heat on my hands. Suddenly, I saw the room. I was on my knees, my palms resting on skin—a blurry blue haze of energy all around. A girl was asleep on her bed—so still, beautiful, awaiting. My eyes closed, I angled forward and felt energy move from above, entering my crown chakra, moving through my neck, shoulders, arms, and hands, connecting to her feet. I felt the vibrations and warmth of this caring energy. I saw the energy move between us.

I carried this body memory with me into the morning. The dream came to me again within the week. I felt more compelled. When it came again, I knew I needed to give the dream more space.

Eventually, Beauty's mutual friend and I met over lunch. LeRae's situation came up, and we talked. I learned about the many people sending prayers and heard about my friend's contribution and experience of helping the healing circle for the young woman. I shared my recurring dream and call to support, knowing the time had come for me to help, and she supported me in this.

Later that same day, I followed up with an email to Beauty, expressing my dream and asking her to ask LeRae if I could come and place my hands on her feet.

A few days later, I received Beauty's response—yes, I could come. In this email, I learned LeRae was healing and that her feet and legs hurt the most.

The next day, I travelled the hour to Saskatoon and made my way to the hospital. I looked for her room. Her room was in the same ward I had spent a week in the year prior. Memories flooded in. I found her room—she was not there. I continued my search and found her downstairs with her father and grandfather, having "an outing"—a visit and a beverage. Gently and with some nervousness, I approached them. I only knew of these people in relation to my new friend Beauty. We chatted for a few moments, and I explained the story of the dream, how I came to be there, and my recent email exchange with Beauty. Then I asked LeRae if she would allow me to spend some time with her and her feet. She said yes. I witnessed how she said goodbye to her grandfather in a loving exchange.

Together, she, her father, and I, made our way up to the hospital room. He helped her get comfortable. I felt privileged to be a witness to the intimacy of these challenging circumstances. Once she was settled and comfortable, he asked if he could leave for a bit. She said yes.

I found a solid position at her feet, and we chatted. She looked beautiful in all her fragility and inherent strength. She was patient and generous with me. I shared with her the circumstances of my daughter's difficult hospital stay a year prior and the impact I felt then. I wanted her to know I was empathetic and wished her connection and safety.

I asked her how she was with "this kind of thing" I was about to do. She was fine and said she had been exposed to many different types of healing before. I asked her if she had a favourite cream I could use for her feet. She showed me where it was. I returned to the end of her bed. I suggested if, during our time together, she noticed colour or if thoughts occurred to her, that she write these observations down or note their presence.

I began with the left foot. I closed my eyes and breathed deeply, allowing the energy to move through and form a dream space to play out for her in her mind. I invited the energy to guide me. I prayed. I felt the fullness of the moment. I felt deep connection with her foot. Kidney, I thought and sent healing energy to those organs. Yes, drink much water, I thought. I felt the intensity of the experience as a resonant energy in my mid-back and kidney area—warm, then hot, much energy streaming, vibrating, and moving. It passed into her ankle and calf. Blue and purple danced. We shared thirty minutes together while I worked on that foot. Then I gently wrapped it and asked for blessings. I moved to her right foot and through a similar process. The experience of shared and shifting energy was profound.

During those moments, I experienced timelessness and formlessness: I am. She is. We are.

My heart believed she would be well. For everyone, it was a time of rest, letting go, receiving, and of purpose yet to be defined. Her experience was a profound gift.

As I carefully wrapped her right foot, the door gently opened. More family came to visit. We exchanged introductions and handshakes. I gifted music to LeRae and asked her to drink lots of water. I also thanked her for sharing time with me and asked her to say hello to her mom. She agreed and seemed tender as we made eye contact. I have much reverence for this young woman who had journeyed so far so early in her life.

A few days later, Beauty emailed me. She was appreciative and shared an update. I shared about the water and kidneys. She said that LeRae was moving to another hospital for a new part of the journey and to just call if I wanted to see her again. I thanked her.

I dream again. Everything was okay. I do not need to go. I sent prayers and loving thoughts and thanked the universe for the opportunity to serve.

I spent some time with Beauty after LeRae came home from the hospital. LeRae was doing well. She and her family had been enriched in wordless ways. I believe only those who give themselves permission to deeply feel, will connect with the heart and spirit energy of this family's journey, particularly the mom and daughter's.

I feel honoured to have shared a small part of their path, and I am glad I committed myself to living holistically in the present and that I followed my dreams and trusted my intuition to be in connection and in the spirit of service.

Two women—they danced together that night. I was moved. So brave, beautiful, and vulnerable they seemed in their generational exchange and gender synchronicity.

To each person in this family who are all "in it together," blessings be into your lives, with gratitude, fellow spirit.

Rod

Mine is a story of two dreams. The first dream occurred fourteen days after LeRae's hospitalization. LeRae was lying in bed, completely motionless with her arms by her side, and because no one had acknowledged me standing next to LeRae's bed, I realized I was an observer in the room. Five young girls entered and sat down on her bed in a U-shaped formation. They were beautiful and had a soft glow about them. Beauty also walked in and passed LeRae's bed to the other side of the room, oblivious to her surroundings and looking like she was in a trance or a deep haze. The five young girls appeared as angels or protectors of LeRae. They also represented a culmination of all the external help being provided to LeRae through prayer, alternative healing, and conventional healing.

The second dream occurred seven days later. I was walking down the street where I grew up as a young child, and a woman, who looked in her sixties, walked passed me. I recognized her as LeRae. She had a little grey hair and a slight limp on her right side. Other than that, she looked completely healthy. This dream showed me that LeRae would ultimately live a full, healthy, happy life.

How did her illness affect me? As an individual I had always been dependent on other people and lacked the personal power to find the answers I needed on my own. Beauty, as one of my spiritual advisers, wasn't available during LeRae's illness, and this forced me to search out my power on my own and begin utilizing it for my own benefit. I was able to see more clearly the dependence I placed on other people, instead of relying on myself to find the answers. The beauty of this experience, I learned, was that while

I could ask for assistance, I was no longer dependent on anyone else for my personal power. This was the gift I felt.

Scott

My wife, God bless her, entertains all my crazy ideas and interests. Many years ago, she gave me a gift certificate to a psychic healing seminar. I was excited to go just to have fun with it. The day of the seminar, I arrived and joined a class of about twenty participants, all of whom, I am sure, were there for all sorts of reasons. The teacher, a self-proclaimed local psychic, greeted everyone and walked us through his background. He believed we all had the ability to be psychics, clairvoyants, healers, dream walkers, or whatever we want, and that we only need to open the right doorway in our minds and focus.

The seminar's agenda was to teach us how to meditate, astral project, read auras, and heal. When we reached the healing segment of the seminar, the teacher asked us to form a circle and hold hands. He proceeded to guide us through a meditation that would relax and clear our minds. After we were relaxed, he asked us to think of someone that might require healing. Well, the only person I could think of was Beauty's daughter LeRae. I thought to myself, I am going to focus as hard as I can and let's just see what happens. Instantly, in my mind's eye, I saw myself, or at least my hands, shooting through the roof and travelling to LeRae's bedside. I couldn't believe how real everything seemed.

As soon as I was beside her, I focused on sending beams of radiating white light out from my hands, filling her and surrounding her. She began to glow, and all I could see was light. This lasted for about five minutes. I am still shocked I was able to hold the image for that long. The instructor guided us back and began to bring us out of the meditation. He finished with a prayer and we discussed our experiences.

I thought the experience was interesting, but that's about it. On the drive home, I called my wife Michelle to let her know I was on my way home. I told her about the things we did and how much fun it was. When I began telling her about the healing circle, she became quiet. When I told her who I was focusing on, she freaked out!

"When did you do the healing circle?" she asked frantically.

"About twenty minutes prior to this call," I responded.

She continued by saying in uncontainable excitement that she had received a call from her mom, Sonia, at that exact time to say LeRae was moving her head and shoulders.

To say the least, we were both extremely excited, not about my experience, but for LeRae. Regardless of whether this healing circle contributed to LeRae's healing, it changed my life. God bless LeRae

Maka

I have known Beauty since May of 2000, and we have maintained a casual friendship, always supporting each other's creative endeavors. The project I was working on at the time was a film that shared the instructions of the prophecy of White Buffalo Calf Woman. It was late autumn 2006, and my journey had brought me to Taos, New Mexico, which was a comfortable place to work on my screenplay. It wasn't an ordinary place—my writing retreat was out on the Three Peaks mesa, where there's no grid. It's a loose community of alternative-minded people who like solar and wind energy systems.

A short walk from the house where I was staying was a Buddhist meditation centre and Tibetan stupa—tall shrines that the Tibetan holy men/lamas are guided to build at certain places of sacred energy. When a person circumambulates the base of the stupa, their prayers become magnified.

On the morning of Saturday November 5, 2006, I was at the sacred site of the Tibetan stupa, and suddenly, I was strongly prompted to give my friend Beauty a call. Her son answered the phone and told me his sister was in the hospital. Her condition sounded serious.

Later that evening, I phoned again and spoke with Beauty herself. She explained that LeRae was in PICU with something called GBS. She also told me that LeRae was now calling in all the people of strong medicine to help her. Beauty said LeRae's Spirit was advising everyone to drop the old samaya of stuck energy that sometimes builds between us, so we could come together as one strong circle of healers.

Beauty shared the timeline of LeRae's sudden illness, and upon reflection, I realized she had begun showing the shocking symptoms of Guillain-Barré Syndrome on an important day. LeRae became ill right after a very powerful ray of light showered the Earth. I learned that subatomic particles are a real phenomenon and that this light is formed when a cosmic ray is emitted by a galaxy going starburst. The October 17 blue-ray energy was announced on the internet at the same time LeRae was moving through her Guillain-Barré illness.

I believe coincidence is the goddess's way of remaining anonymous. The poetess in me is tickled—cosmic blue ray, LeRae, Guillain-Barré! Who dreamt this scenario? As a shamanic practitioner, I interpreted that LeRae and her family were going through a form of initiation with her intense, deathlike illness.

Traditionally, shamans were buried alive as an initiation test of their powers. Interestingly, as we, LeRae's healers, offered our best medicine to bring LeRae out of illness into health, many of us were given the opportunity to practice holding the positive vibration, just as it was prescribed in the blue-ray cosmic event.

Thank you, LeRae, Beauty, Ed, and Austin for awakening my compassion and encouraging me to practice my best medicine for the tribe during these amazing times of transition for Mother Earth. Many blessings.

Craig

Our souls are more informed than our minds. Our challenges serve as veils covering truth. If we are strong enough and willing to reach for the message within the challenge, we can overcome anything that tries to erase our purpose. So, what of a mother's brave heart? As deep and red as any beating heart, in the face of death, she can lend her thoughts to the innocent, so they may borrow her courage or her fear. Which shall it be? The weak cannot choose the strength or resolve to manifest life. They must wither, and they must die so that the strong will pass the world to a future that is brighter and more compassionate.

I witnessed a tremendous amount of courage and calm in desperate times by knowing that fear would shed its shaking skin. Life would push forth from the fertile earth of a mother's vision for complete recovery and a father's quiet determination to hold firm to the path of support through all tides of discouragement and hopelessness. He who holds up mountains so his children can pass through, so his life's partner can travel her path, so others will benefit from his great, undying strength of purpose and service to the life givers of the earth. The mothers, the daughters, and the sons lend their strength to that which uncovers the veil and allows life to replace both death's withered greyness and the unresolved gifts that may die with it. I salute and honour you both. I thank you for blessing the world with your many and splendid gifts!

Dolphyn

My name is Dolphyn Boschman. I have been a certified holistic health practitioner for over twenty years and a good friend of Beauty's for more than a decade. When Beauty first told me LeRae was in the hospital with a serious condition because of an autoimmune disease, I found the whole thing surreal. How could GBS take a perfectly healthy young teenager and commit her to a ventilating machine and paralysis.

Once I was over the shock, I knew my response would be the same as if LeRae had a simple cold or a deadly virus. First, I needed to hold the vision for what I wanted. I believe we create and manifest everything in our lives for a reason. What we give our attention to creates the energy that manifests our results. So, my focus had to be the certainty that LeRae would get through her ordeal.

At that time, I was doing a lot of yoga and practicing focused intent. My instructor would lead us by asking us to focus on our own practice, while holding in our minds and hearts someone to also do our practice for—the intention. As we inhaled, we draw in the other's exhale. As we exhale, the other inhales our essence/gifts we are exhaling.

While LeRae was in the hospital, I did my practice for Beauty. She was/ is my soul sister and I knew she would feel my energy immediately. I also knew she would need an abundance of energy to help LeRae through the process and to deal with the often negative energy that surrounds trauma, hospitals, Western medicine, etc.

Here is an excerpt from an email I sent Beauty in 2006, after one of those yoga sessions:

> *We did a Tibetan Heart Yoga practice tonight. First, we did a meditation by visualizing a rose (or lotus) at our heart and a diamond at our third eye. We then drew the diamond to rest in the flower. We then visualized the other person's pain gathering to their heart as a dark ball. As we inhaled, we drew it out of the person until it was completely gone. We then inhaled it into our body to our heart where, once it touched the diamond, it exploded in a burst of golden fireworks, destroyed forever. We then began our practice by sending six gifts to the recipient to heal and replace the pain. Each pose represented a different gift to give to the one in need. By inhaling the gift itself (one word) and exhaling with the affirmation.*
>
> *The Tibetan gifts are:*
>
> *1. I give you the gift of Giving*
> *2. I give you the gift of Kindness*
> *3. I give you the gift of Patience*
> *4. I give you the gift of Joy*
> *5. I give you the gift of Stillness*
> *6. I give you the gift of Wisdom*

So, darling Beauty, I hope you could see and feel me sitting in front of you, willing to take on your pain, and that you could feel the gifts of the Universe that are made yours simply by placing your attention on them and breathing them in. I love you very much, Goddess, and I will not feed the pain or negativity by focusing on it or feeling hopelessness or despair. I will be your strength, love, healing, compassion, and peace.

I don't want you to think I am making light of the situation. I am not! We are goddesses and play by different rules. I must be careful of where I put my attention, what I focus on, and what I attract. I only want to attract a positive outcome for you and your family. You are too dear to me, all of you.

Beauty

If, for one second, I, or any of the above people, would have questioned what we were hearing or being guided to do, or if we'd cared what other people thought (especially me, who brought healer after healer to LeRae's bedside), this story would have ended differently.

Thank you to everyone who heard LeRae's call and for taking immediate action, openly and anonymously. Your gracious offering of time, energy, and prayers gave LeRae the opportunity to continue drawing from the infinite well of source energy, filling her with what she needed to lift herself back into her own light.

Bless you all.

Ten
Bare Bones

Beauty

My mom Carol loves writing notes. I was unaware that she'd documented LeRae's daily highs and lows in the hospital until I asked her to write her story. She then handed me her notes. After I read them, I realized their significance and decided to include them in this book. At first, my mom was hesitant to agree, especially when I said I wanted to leave them as is—raw and unedited. I strongly felt that editing her notes would ultimately take away from the matter-of-fact account of her granddaughter's life-threatening illness. It also captivates LeRae's journey brilliantly.

Notes by Nana

October 2006–March 2007

October 20, 2006—Ed phones us in Ontario where we are vacationing and leaves a message . . . we start our drive home. We are told that LeRae has been given an IVIG transfusion (plasma protein replacement therapy)—a treatment for severely affected patients and a strong sedative.

October 21—More information from home . . . LeRae had a good sleep but can only open one eye and still has double vision.

October 22—We arrive back in Saskatoon at 4:00 p.m. and go straight to the hospital. LeRae is unable to open her eyes but she can hear very well and only one person is permitted in the room. It was a heartbreaking experience to see her that way . . . we told her how much we loved her and that we would be there for her and to fight as hard as she could to get better.

October 24—Crystal and Shalene visit with news about school. I am almost finished reading the story "Hacker" which is corny but amusing for us, I think.

October 25—I am reading another story to LeRae, I am four chapters in and it was doctor time again. Beauty arrived at 1:00 p.m. and LeRae was sleeping. Ed arrived after work and began rubbing LeRae's neck and back trying to make her more comfortable . . . communication is difficult. Tillie arrived at 8:00 p.m. and gave LeRae some "healing energy." LeRae's cold has developed into pneumonia giving her another battle to fight! Bells go off whenever LeRae's blood pressure goes up or something else triggers the equipment—perhaps she is trying to let us know that she needs something, it is then that we do our best to communicate with her by lifting an eyelid, so she can move her eye in answer to the questions—which I imagine is frustrating for her when we aren't asking the right questions!

October 26—I arrived at 10:30 a.m. Ed was massaging her forehead. Ed and the nurse moved LeRae again to try and make her more comfortable. She can now twitch her left eyelash a wee bit and her breathing is improving but she definitely needs the ventilators help. The nurse is pounding on her chest again, trying to break up the congestion—it is necessary yet hard to watch so I had to leave the room.

October 28—More family and friends visit. LeRae is given some meds and sleeps seven hours, which is needed.

October 29—Tillie visits along with Aunt Judy.

October 30—Crystal and Jessica visit and bring a big stuffed animal and a card with wishes from her school friends. It's 10:00 p.m. and all of a sudden LeRae's heart is beating fast and scaring everyone—drugs are administered to calm her down.

October 31—10:00 a.m. Ed is there along with the heart physicians who are doing an ECG, they say LeRae has a good strong heart and not to worry. More specialists arrive throughout the day. She is like a pin cushion with so many IVs. The braces on her teeth are causing some discomfort so they are removing them—she was to get them removed in January anyway. Judy visited and LeRae nodded a little and everyone was thrilled. LeRae's doctor is going to start her on steroids to speed her recovery.

November 1—LeRae is trying to open one eye a little. I read the card the kids had sent from school. LeRae moved her left shoulder a wee bit and I told her again how proud we all were of her for being so strong.

November 2—The braces were removed this morning and MRI done at 11:30 a.m. LeRae now has an airbed.

November 3—LeRae's eyes are swollen. Her mega doses of Prednisone have started and last for four days. Her physiotherapy from bed also starts today. Blood pressure skyrockets again but possibly because she is trying to breathe on her own. Ed and Beauty reassure LeRae that the ventilator machine is her friend and will not abandon her when she is trying to breathe on her own.

November 4—Debbie's sister Brenda came from Winnipeg with a "get well" card from her class, a teddy bear and a c.d. filled with well-wishes. Both Beauty and I were moved by this gesture as they do not know our family but were praying for LeRae's recovery. Tillie spent 1 ½ hours with LeRae. G.G. arrived and LeRae was able to open her right eye half way which made G.G. very happy to see.

November 5—Ventilator is now at -7 which means LeRae is breathing a little on her own. LeRae is having a bad day today as her throat is very sore from the tube and when she has to swallow it hurts, then causes her to gag.

November 6—LeRae can now move her head enough so she has more control and not gagging as much.

November 7—Austin came to visit at 11 a.m. and read some jokes from his "knock knock" book. The nurses have put a movie on and propped LeRae up in bed—they are challenging her to open her eyes and be in different positions.

Beauty is busy massaging LeRae's legs again. Ed arrived when I was there, and he said, "well honey, how did your day go?" LeRae opened her right eye and rolled it upward and as if to read her mind Ed said: "I know, the pits—but it's going to get better!"

November 8—LeRae communicated that she had a burning sensation in her body that was about a number seven, so meds were given. Her urine sample came back abnormal, now checking for Porphyria—what next!

November 9—The doctors don't agree on the porphyria result and are instead giving a second round of IVIG. Ed is trying to communicate by using the alphabet. He says the letters and LeRae communicates when to stop—it's a slow process spelling out the words and she tries with her lower lip to say stop but it's hard for us to figure out and must be frustrating for her. She continues to get morphine for the pain she is having so it makes her dopey.

November 10—I spent most of the day with LeRae as Beauty was with Austin and Ed was working. LeRae has spelled out the word "cold" and I guessed what she wanted for the first time . . . a cold cloth on her forehead. Beauty arrived in the afternoon and Ed will arrive later.

November 11—I have a touch of laryngitis so I cannot read to LeRae. Ed was able to move one of LeRae's arms and legs a bit but her one leg is quite swollen.

November 12—A rough day!!! LeRae has a fever, urinary infection and quite a few choking episodes. She also had a leg infection causing her leg to swell. Doriana visits and wonders why she doesn't have a PIC line, she makes an inquiry and spurs some action.

November 13—LeRae's fever broke in the a.m. and Travis is doing some physio. Doctors checked breathing power again and it is now at -20 (up from -7) and when it gets to -30 or -40, the ventilating tube is removed. Crystal and Keejara visit and LeRae is always glad to see her friends. Austin came and brought a black teddy bear. I was happy to see her sitting up a bit, opening one eye and smiling. What a trouper she is.

November 14—LeRae gets the PIC line today. LeRae was able to communicate to Ed that she wanted to know what was wrong with her as she couldn't remember. He explained what GBS was and that it was a slow recovery, but she was doing very well.

November 15—LeRae woke at 3:00 a.m. and was coughing and choking. Beauty arrived first thing in the morning and was able to calm her down. Travis arrives for physio. She sits on the edge of the bed and keeps her back straight and is able to hold her head up a bit by herself. When the physio is done she gets sick and has to have her throat suctioned.

November 16—LeRae blew a -37 today!

November 17—LeRae didn't sleep well and was throwing up at 5:00 a.m. Travis arrived and did physio while she was laying down. LeRae was sick throughout the day and when I arrived Ed said she just had an "hour of hell." Ed is staying the night.

November 18—HALLELUJAH DAY! LeRae is breathing on her own, she had to wear a mask with oxygen and moisture for about five hours along with a contraption on her nose. Austin and I were sure happy to see her breathing on her own.

November 19—LeRae is moved across the hall to the General Ward into 3015 Observation. LeRae still isn't sleeping well. G.G. visited and was overjoyed to see her and hear a few whispers.

November 20—LeRae didn't sleep well again. Travis had to wake her up for physio at 10:00 a.m. She is also dealing with another urinary infection and needs to suck up the pain as she cannot have any morphine until 2:00 p.m. and it is only noon.

November 21—LeRae's catheter was taken out today as she was in excruciating pain

November 22—No physio today, LeRae was too tired . . . no sleep the night before because the patient sharing the room was sick all night. LeRae also had a swallowing test and then had to sit in the physiotherapy chair for one hour. She can have soft food now but eating means pooping and that is difficult for her because her bowels aren't fully working yet.

November 23—Another HALLELUJAH DAY! . . . the feeding tube is removed . . . one yank and it was out . . . shocked all of us. LeRae can now start eating different foods.

November 24—LeRae visited with her friends today on the main floor and fell asleep for a bit while they were talking to her. Her feet are bothering her now and the pain causes her to cry.

November 25—LeRae sets a goal to be home for Christmas!

November 26—Papa arrived, and he cried tears of happiness when LeRae showed him all that she could do. She also had a visit from a family friend who had GBS who was encouraging. However, when he left, LeRae cried because she missed her friends and wished they could visit more often.

November 27—LeRae is able to eat whatever she wants like french fries, pasta and rolo ice cream. She is also able to cover and uncover herself with the blanket.

November 28—LeRae is able to feed herself yogurt but can't manage the soup by herself because of the shaking. LeRae is able to communicate with her friends now on the computer through MSN, very slowly though.

November 29—She stood by herself (with help) beside her bed but couldn't feel her feet . . . Travis was very impressed.

November 30—LeRae moved from Observation to room 3023. She is now able to go to the physiotherapy room and is off morphine and everyone is happy about that.

December 1—LeRae is on the waiting list to go to City Hospital Rehab.

December 2—G.G. and Aunt Judy visit and are excited with LeRae's progress. She is able to bend her knees and move her hips.

December 5—One hour of physiotherapy today and she is learning how to move in the wheelchair.

December 6—Many visitors today. LeRae is able to feed herself soup and eat carrots. She is also happy as she can blow her own nose and wipe it too! Every little accomplishment is a big one for her.

December 10—I took LeRae some scrapbooking supplies and she is making cards.

December 12—LeRae is going to City Hospital for physiotherapy in the pool.

December 14—LeRae is moved to City Hospital room 7235 . . . it is bright and quiet. Next week she starts physio 3x per week, plus some school work.

December 17—PaPa visited her today and she dropped a pencil on the floor and bent over to pick it up but said "ouch" as it hurt but he was impressed with her progress.

December 19—I picked LeRae and Beauty up at 1:30 p.m. from City Hospital . . . OT and PT therapists were doing an assessment of the house since she was still in a wheelchair.

December 22—YEAH!!! I picked LeRae and Beauty up at 1:30 p.m. . . . she gets to stay home until Wednesday at 10:00 a.m.

December 23—One of LeRae's friends sleeps over

December 24—The whole family went to church on Christmas Eve and everyone was happy to see her.

December 25—A 'WOW' day . . . LeRae's goal was to be home for Christmas!!!!!!

December 26—Another friend sleeps over.

December 27—Physiotherapy at City Hospital.

December 31—New Year's Eve . . . Crystal came over and we all played board games and had lots of laughs.

January 1, 2007—Back to City Hospital.

January 3—ANOTHER HALLELUJAH DAY . . . LeRae is coming home. I pick her and Beauty up at 4:00 p.m. along with all of her stuff. Travis from RUH drops by to wish her a speedy recovery and gives her a big hug—he is very nice.

January 7—LeRae moves back to her bedroom in the basement, she scoots down the stairs on her bum and gets up that way too—her arms are becoming really strong.

January 11–13—It's the annual basketball tournament at Bedford Road Collegiate and Ed took her on Thursday and Beauty on Friday. She was still in her wheelchair.

January–February—LeRae's journey continues. She continues her therapy at City Hospital as an outpatient. She is now going to school in her wheelchair.

February 16—LeRae is now moving around on her knees which is helping to strengthen the muscles in her upper legs. She still cannot feel much in her feet— they are numb.

February 17—LeRae is using a walker.

March 4—LeRae has braces for her feet and legs to help keep them aligned when she is using the walker.

March 13—LeRae visits the doctor who first saw her when she was admitted to PICU at Royal University Hospital. He was excited about her recovery thus far and shared with her how frightened he had been as she was so sick. He told her that she must exercise her feet, especially the toes if she wants to walk without the supports. He also said her mind would need to retrain her feet to know what to do . . . being as strong willed as she is, there is no doubt in my mind that she will recover, even though it may be a slow process.

March 27—HALLELUJAH DAY . . . LeRae went to school with her cane—no wheelchair . . . she wears leg braces. She had her 'bodyguard' friends watching over her as she moved from class to class.

Eleven

Rising Free

LeRae

I remember how amazing it felt to sleep in my own bed after I was discharged from the hospital. The overwhelming feeling of being connected to the higher power my mom had talked about since I was a little girl was incredible. Most of the time she referred to this higher power as *God*, and sometimes she would use other words like *Universe* or *Great Spirit*. I never really understood what she meant by higher power, until I had to fight for my life. It felt like I was being blessed and protected by an invisible source that made me feel safe and invincible. This feeling contributed to my ability to continue accomplishing things that were said to be impossible. It also influenced my decision to live my life fearlessly. By my sixteenth birthday, I was living my life so fearlessly that my parents had to step in to set me straight.

I remember my mom saying, "There's a difference between living fearlessly and living recklessly and, right now, you're living recklessly."

She reminded me that my reckless behaviour was a blessing and was directly related to my GBS experience. I didn't realize I was unconsciously putting myself in unsafe situations and unhealthy relationships to heal. She helped me understand how my wildest emotional outbursts were directly linked to the emotions I'd suppressed while I was ventilated. She also shared a personal truth: every relationship, circumstance, and dramatic event being presented to me was for me, rather than against me. I was attracting exactly what I needed to crack open what was buried deep inside and maybe, one day, I would be grateful for the experiences.

My emotional turmoil and get-out-of-my-way attitude spun out of control. I remember my parents waiting patiently for the day when I realized I needed help. They knew I had to make that choice on my own. The first call my mom made was to Tillie, who recommended a female therapist specializing in post-traumatic stress disorder. During my sessions with her, I consciously released my suppressed anger, which enabled me to become more emotionally stable. My life transformed. I was happy, healthy, and enjoying all the things I used to do and more. I was singing, snowboarding, travelling, and finishing my diploma in therapeutic recreation. To top it all off, I started dancing again. At first, it was just for fun, but as I continued to improve Kimberly Parent, the director of Saskatoon Salsa Dance Company, asked me to join their performance team.

Years later, self-sabotaging thoughts slowly became my mind's focus. I began feeling more afraid than safe. I stopped going to the gym, eating healthy, and appreciating my body. My hamstring and calf muscles ached constantly and became so tight that I created a mild version of planter fasciitis, limiting the abilities I had worked so hard to rebuild in my recovery. Though difficult, I had to admit I was taking my body and life for granted again. I knew I needed help, so I asked my mom for a healing session. For as long as I can remember, she's been offering me a variety of healing methods, depending on my needs. After each session, she's often said, "My love, this is what your soul wants you to know. I am simply the messenger. You always have the choice to do with it as you will."

Sometimes, I understood exactly what she was saying and other times, I didn't have a clue. I've learned to apply what feels right and let go of what doesn't. She's taught me that as well. She also continuously reminds me that I'm the only one who has the power to choose how I will respond to life's circumstances. Only I choose how I feel, the thoughts I think, and what I believe. No one else chooses this for me unless I let them. My first step to becoming aware of this mindset was to practice *becoming*, or, what she calls, being *consciously conscious*—becoming aware of my thoughts by paying attention to what I'm thinking and asking, whether these are my thoughts or are they thoughts coming from an outside source, like social media. The moment I started practicing bringing my attention to my own thoughts, I realized how negative I was being towards myself and others. At first, I was hard on myself and felt guilty for having these thoughts. My mom reminded me that becoming consciously conscious is a day-to-day practice and that loving myself through it is essential. This was a powerful realization, which I continue to practice to this day.

After the healing session, she offered me what she calls a "soul prescription." This prescription included several options I could choose from: Reiki, myofascial massage treatments, and daily yoga topped the list. I intuitively knew, to heal myself, I needed to listen to her advice and start taking care of myself again. I began doing self-Reiki and daily yoga. I also booked sessions with Tillie and a myofascial massage therapist. I also changed my eating habits by making healthier food choices. My body became stronger, my mind became calmer, and once again I was accomplishing things I was told I would never be able to do.

Surprise, surprise, another self-healing journey was awakened within me after I began writing this book. As I wrote about my experiences, I realized I wasn't sure what or who God was for me anymore. My life was full, and I was content with how it was moving forward, yet I had an unsettling feeling that I didn't understand until I began writing about my experience. I had lost my love, strength, and faith somewhere along the way, and I didn't know how to find them. I was confused and frustrated. It didn't feel right to call God, *God* anymore, not until I understood what it meant for me.

I became extremely hard on myself again. After everything I'd overcome, I felt like I should know what I believed in, and I definitely felt like I should be making more of a difference in the world. I shared my feelings with my mom, and she tearfully replied: "Oh my gosh, LeRae, you make a difference just by being here, by being you. Everywhere you go, your being-ness and life experiences affect everything and everyone around you, whether you're aware of it or not. When you laid your body down, so your soul could heal, the rest of us received our own profound healing as well. Your journey with GBS changed people's lives in ways you may never comprehend. It transcended logic into the miraculous and that, my love, was your gift. Now that you are sharing your journey by writing this book, you will again be making a difference for the people who choose to read it."

My mom knew I was experiencing another soul shift and encouraged me to be open to the new information being awakened within me. As I allowed her words to sink into my soul, a familiar sensation gently began to fill my body. I was remembering the tranquil feeling I felt while recovering from GBS. I remember asking my mom while I was in the hospital about this tranquil feeling, and she adamantly said, "That is called grace my love, and you are swimming in it."

This was the feeling I was missing. As I allowed myself to feel this sensation again, I was able to reconnect with my feelings of love, strength, and faith. I began to feel more peaceful and balanced. I understood that grace comes from within; I just need to remember to feel it. I also became aware of why I stopped allowing myself to truly love anything, including myself. I discovered how devastating it had been to have everything ripped away from me when I became ill. This ultimately made me feel I had lost my way. I had created a wall of protection around my heart to keep me from feeling that kind of pain again. I was afraid to open my heart and fully love, because the thought of it being ripped away was terrifying. I shared my feelings with my mom.

"My love, it is just as painful to hold your love in as it is to fully love, and have it ripped away. In my experience both can be devastating and equally painful. The moment you become conscious of this, you have a choice—to love fully and risk the pain of losing it or love empty and feel nothing. This is the dance of life."

I chose to love and feel again. The moment I made that choice, the universe opened and showed me everything I needed. I signed up for a workshop called Desire Mapping through Kari Hollingsworth and started doing exercises from two books; *The Artist's Way* and *The Magic*. These choices ignited a fire within me that cracked open my fragile, wounded heart.

The first conscious choice I made, was to reconnect with the fifteen-year-old girl that carried me through my illness. I didn't realize I'd left her behind until my mom decided to facilitate a workshop called Illuminated Voice ~ Dancing Spirit. It was a six-week course that focused on sacred sound, free-form movement, and chakra toning. The third week was all about the heart chakra. My mom guided us through a visual meditation so we could each connect with our little girl inside. She asked us to move into a comfortable position, place our hands over our hearts, and to close our eyes. As she guided us through the exercise, an image of a closed door appeared in my mind, then slowly opened, and a bright light started to shine through the cracks. Suddenly, I saw my own little face peeking out from behind the door. She was hesitant to come out. I let her know everything was going to be okay and that she was safe now. She stepped out from behind the door wearing a hospital gown with a took-you-long-enough smirk on her face. Tears of gratitude flowed, as I wept for her and for me. I was finally able to embrace her and set her free. I realized she was always there, waiting patiently for me to come find her.

I can honestly say I will never be the same person I was before my illness. My journey with GBS brought me to a new place within myself. I found a new *love* and appreciation for my family, friends, and people who were there for me. I also uncovered an inner, unwavering *strength* and a renewed *faith* in God, in healing, in medicine and in trusting what will be, will be.

I understand I was destined to go through this journey to become who I am today. Before my illness I moved fast and had little patience. Today, there is a slow and steady pace in my world and within myself. On days I forget, my mom's words echo in my mind: *The gift in my forgetting is that I'm able to have the amazing experience of remembering.* I'm able to remember what I've been through, how important my breath truly is, and to cherish my life. That feeling is incredible.

If I ever lose sight of who I am again, I'll be able to come back to these pages and remember. Some days it feels like it was another life, as if it were another person who went through this life-changing experience. Well, it wasn't. It was me. I was able to rise from my near-death experience and overcome the impossible. I fought, I surrendered, and I conquered.

Twelve
Beauty Indigo Blue

Beauty

I knew I wanted to be a mother from an early age. How did I know? I always volunteered to be the mommy, instead of the baby, when I played make believe with my friends. I also remember finding injured animals, mostly birds, and nurturing them back to health, as if they were my own children. As I grew older, I became a passionate protector, fearlessly standing up for my friends and my younger brother. I was seven years old when my brother Curtis was born, and the moment my parents brought him home from the hospital, I decided he was my son instead of my brother. I had fun pretending to be his mommy, for a while, and as he grew older, I stepped into the role of his fiercely protective sister.

Meeting Ed, my husband was no different. From the first moment I saw him, I felt a weird, tingling sensation move in and around my heart. I knew then, he would be my husband one day, although I didn't understand how this would happen, since I was only eleven, and I didn't even like him at the time. His way of interacting with me was to chase me, pull my hair, and shove my face in the snow. He finally admitted that the only reason he was doing those things was because he liked me.

The first time he asked me to be his girlfriend was in grade eight. I was surprised and a bit hesitant to say yes because of his previous actions towards me. I had developed strong feelings for him, yet was confused as to why I had them. I said yes anyway. We dated for a few months until I decided we needed to part ways. It was difficult at first to see each other at school, but we did our best to remain friends. After our grade eight graduation, we didn't see each other again until the first day of grade nine. Talk about a magnetic pull! I had no clue why that pull was still there—it just was. Nevertheless, he was in a relationship, so I let it be, which meant I stuffed my feelings. Supressing my feelings worked for a while, until he started to show up wherever I was. I ignored him at first, which, in turn, made him try harder to get my attention. Eventually, he let me know he was single and that he wanted me to be his girlfriend again. I was excited and somewhat afraid to say yes since the girl he'd just broken up with was in grade ten, popular, and had many friends. I told him the only way I'd agree to be his girlfriend was if we kept it quiet until I was ready to tell people, and he said okay. We met secretly for about three weeks, and, when we finally decided to share our secret, no one was surprised. It turned out, we weren't doing a good job of hiding it anyway. We dated all through high school and were married on May 12, 1984.

Six years later, we decided to expand our family. I was elated and eager to put into practice what I believed was my calling. I was quite shocked, when, after becoming pregnant with LeRae, I began vomiting uncontrollably. I felt like it was never going to end. One evening, before I crawled into bed, I placed a letter under my pillow addressed to God. I asked forgiveness for whatever I'd done to cause such extreme sickness for something I believed was my calling.

I was raised with a mix of religious teachings: Protestant through my birth family, primarily via my mother, and Roman Catholic through my Italian caregivers, whom I considered my family. In my younger years, I loved learning about God, the Bible, and the teachings of Jesus through these two interconnected religions. By the time I became a teenager, I was completely confused and filled with fear. I didn't realize I was learning these teachings literally. I actually believed I would be struck by lightning if I didn't follow the rules or make good choices. At fifteen, this was an impossible task. Many times, I believed I wouldn't see the light of day because of some choice I'd made. Jay walking, for example, would send me on a wild ride of inner punishment. I had a similar guilt-ridden mindset when I wrote the letter to God about my situation.

The night I placed the letter under my pillow, I had a dream filled with translucent white light. A silhouette of a man with his arms stretched out appeared before me. He said, "I am Jesus. I am here to lift you into the light. There is nothing you could ever do to keep me from loving you." I woke from the dream, leaned over, and calmly asked Ed to drive me to emergency. I was admitted for ten days and diagnosed with hyperemesis graviderum, which includes severe nausea and vomiting, leading to possible dehydration. As soon as the vomiting subsided, I went home.

LeRae arrived on June 13, 1991. Giving birth to a beautiful healthy baby girl felt like a miracle. I remember feeling an indescribable love pulse through my entire body the moment she was born. I was ready to be the awesome mother I believed I was destined to be. Surprisingly, the daily responsibilities of taking care of her became overwhelming. I was so concerned with keeping her safe and handling her with extreme care that I began to doubt my mothering abilities. She was six pounds three ounces, with no fat on her tiny body. She was also colicky and didn't sleep well for the first three months. Many times, I felt I was going to lose my mind trying to figure out how to calm her down. Finally, in the early hours of the morning, while cuddling her and praying for a solution, the answer came: *ask for help.*

I first asked for advice from my mother, then other mothers who had already moved through the newborn phase. I then purchased numerous books about parenting, which helped me gain valuable knowledge. Five years later, Austin was born. He came in at six pounds eleven ounces, with a bit more fat on his bones than LeRae. He was healthy, adorable, and cute, just like LeRae. By the time he was born, my confidence in my mothering abilities had increased substantially, and my experience with him, as a new born, was considerably less stressful. Thankfully, he came into the world more like a lamb than a lion, and his temperament always reflected this.

Through my experience with LeRae, who had come into the world like a lion, I learned a valuable lesson: most of her distress was directly related to my distress. My thoughts of worry and fear, along with my lack of self-confidence, were contributing to her spirited behaviour. Asking for help and applying what I was learning from all the books I was reading was immensely beneficial. The more I practiced the recommended exercises within each book, the calmer I became, and so did LeRae. It was amazing to witness her spirited behaviour transform effortlessly into a peaceful state, as I consciously chose the feeling of peace while I was in her presence.

My new awareness that my thoughts, feelings, and beliefs could directly affect me, and ripple out to the people around me, including my children, was life changing. It awakened within me an unwavering desire to become one hundred percent responsible for my energy, my thoughts, and my feelings. Ultimately, this desire became a pivotal marker within my own inner quest for self-realization.

Fast forward to my thirty-third birthday on December 29, 1997: I was happily married, raising two beautiful children while working full-time as a medical office assistant, and training for another body-building competition. I was thriving and loved what I was doing. I was also intensely focused on being super at everything—super mom, wife, employee, daughter, friend, sister, etc.—and I believed I was pulling it off in spades.

Three months later, I began experiencing a tingling sensation on the inside of my right foot, and, when I used the gym's step-climbing machine, my entire foot would become numb. I chose to simply ignore it and hoped the pain would go away. Eventually, the painful tingling sensation moved into my left foot, up both my legs, and into my hips, the pain became overwhelming and I had to leave my full-time job. Thankfully, I was offered a part-time position at the chiropractic clinic where I was receiving treatments for the pain. I promptly accepted the position. As the pain worsened, it manifested into a chronic condition. My legs felt like they were on fire, yet they were cold to the touch, and my toes would turn blue.

My family doctor referred me to a variety of specialists, who tried their best to diagnose me. None could pinpoint the problem, and I ended up being misdiagnosed and moderately medicated. Modern medicine was all I knew at that time, and prescription medication had always worked for me in the past. This time was different. None of them were working, and my mystery pain continued. Finally, the chronic pain forced me to quit the part-time job I adamantly wanted to keep. I didn't realize I was holding a limiting, subconscious belief that equated quitting with failing. I thought my only option was to push through the pain, even though my physical body was screaming, stop!

On my last day at the chiropractic office, the doctor, who had become my mentor, pulled me aside and quietly asked, "Do you know what Reiki is?"

"No," I said.

"Would you like to?"

"Sure," I eagerly replied.

He proceeded to direct me towards the examining room and asked me to sit on the chair in front of him.

"Please close your eyes," he softly said, as he gently placed one hand on either side of my ears. He held his hands in this position for about fifteen minutes. I could feel the heat from his hands flow through my entire body, and I started to cry. He said that my tears were a good sign and to let them flow.

"Is it alright to share what I'm seeing?"

"Yes," I whispered.

"I see your body wrapped tightly like a mummy, with cloth and twine. When I placed my hands over your ears, the cloth and twine unravelled. This is also a good sign. It means Reiki will help you."

After he finished, he handed me a card with his Reiki master's phone number on it and encouraged me to contact her. At the time, it was all too weird and too out of the box for me to grasp, so I simply thanked him and said goodbye.

I knew the decision to finally quit my job was necessary if I was to have any chance of becoming well. It also meant facing the chronic pain and emotional turmoil in the privacy of my own home. I discovered, through trial and error, what eased my pain and what amplified it. Having a bath and, surprisingly, watching television eased it. After this wonderful discovery, I began bathing three to four times a day—a hot bath followed by a cold one. This enabled my body to relax, which alleviated my pain substantially. For a short time, watching television became a welcome distraction. It gave me the opportunity to stop focusing on my pain, which in turn made me feel less pain. It was also the catalyst that introduced me to The Oprah Show. The show's format was based on helping others find inner peace through self-love, acceptance, and gratitude. I instantly fell in love with her authentic nature, no-nonsense attitude, and genuine care for others. I began to faithfully watch her show and read all the books she endorsed. I had already seen nine specialists and was about to see the tenth, when my incredible liberating experience occurred. The specialist was a neurologist with a long waiting list, and I'd waited three months to see him.

"Well my dear, there's nothing physically wrong with you. It's emotional," he said confidently, as he completed his examination.

"Emotional—what do you mean?" I replied.

He proceeded to tell me he'd just arrived back from Africa and was introduced to "a different kind of medicine." He called it alternative holistic medicine.

"Have you heard of it?" he asked.

"No," I said, "What is that?"

He suggested I do some research at the public library and go from there. He also strongly advised that I find a new path, since the one I was on was going nowhere.

"My dear" he said, "There's nothing I or anyone can do for you. This is something you must heal within yourself."

His radical honesty was shocking and life changing. As soon as I started researching and asking questions about alternative holistic medicine, I realized I'd already introduced myself to some of it through The Oprah Show. Even though I was making progress and feeling hopeful, the chronic pain continued. During another lonely, painful afternoon, my out-of-control fearful thoughts, created a dark, dreary place in my mind, and I contemplated ending my life. I remember yelling out loud, "God, please, there must be another way out of this pain other than ending my life. Please, show me what that is. My children need me."

Call Bryan. One minute I was yelling out loud, the next minute I was rolling over, picking up the phone, and calling Bryan. He was one of the myofascial massage therapists helping me deal with my chronic pain who had become one of my spiritual advisers. He listened intently to my desperate plea.

"You're having a spiritual emergency. You need to take Rescue Remedy, lay down, and listen to the voice deep inside you," he calmly stated.

"Okay," I said softly and hung up the phone.

I had no idea what Rescue Remedy was or how I was going to find it. I was also in no shape to drive a vehicle. Suddenly, the doorbell rang. I didn't want to see anyone, yet something within me knew I needed to answer the door. It was my mother-in-law. She said she was in the neighborhood and needed to drop something off. I accepted the package with my everything-was-fine façade and then, as she was leaving, I simply asked her if she had time to go to the local health food store and pick up something called Rescue Remedy. Moments later, she was on her way. When she arrived back to the house, she handed me a tiny paper bag and said goodbye. I thanked her and closed the door.

I quickly opened the paper bag, grabbed the tiny bottle from inside, read the directions, and applied ten to fifteen drops under my tongue. I laid on my bed, closed my eyes, and breathed deeply, just as Bryan had suggested. About thirty minutes later, I noticed my dark thoughts were disappearing, and I was moving into a more peaceful state of my mind. The spiritual emergency that Bryan had intuitively diagnosed me with swiftly turned into a spiritual awakening. This was when I experienced my first vision. It was powerful, moving, and offered me profound insight into my deeply despairing situation. As the vision faded, I heard, *I love you. There is nothing wrong. Embrace thyself,* and I began to weep. Instead of feeling sad, I felt a heaviness lift from my heart and a glimmer of hope emerge from within me, which was enough to motivate me to take action.

I became tenacious and diligently committed to embracing the light instead of focusing on the darkness. To do that, I needed to wake up from the shadowland I had created within myself. The strong, fit, muscular physique I spent years building had atrophied, leaving me weak, full of pain, and unable to walk.

One evening, as I was laying on the living room floor, looking up at the ceiling, I heard, *Turn the music on.* I crawled over to the CD player and turned it on— "Ray of Light" by Madonna began to play. I laid back down on the floor in Savasana[10] and allowed the music to fill my body. Then something amazing happened: my arms and legs began moving effortlessly to the music, which created a beautiful outlet for my body to release the pain. This new form of organic pain relief became my daily medicine. I would begin in Savasana then allow my body to move freely to an eclectic mix of music for as long as I needed to. Eventually, as time passed, I made my way onto all fours, and finally into a standing position. I call this spirit dancing. The more I surrendered and let go of control, the more I became one with the music. For me, spirit dancing became an exhilarating, ecstatic, free-flowing, whole-body experience. My body began to move with the

---

[10] Lying on the back, with arms and legs spread at about 45 degrees, the eyes are closed, and the breath is deep.

flow of my soul as it sang the songs of my life story. It was incredible. I was able to release my suppressed emotions, strengthen my body, and begin practicing yoga. I also continued to meditate, visualize myself vibrant and healthy, and faithfully watch The Oprah Show. Only when I tried another homeopathic remedy, recommended by a reputable homeopathic doctor, was I able to finally access the source of my chronic pain. On my first visit, after completing a thorough assessment of my life history, he recommended a remedy that would assist me in peeling away all the layers of my past. He advised me to begin with a low dose and work my up to a stronger one.

Ultimately, this remedy became the catalyst for the unveiling of my deepest wounds, fear-driven thoughts, past-life memories, and unresolved feelings. The deeper I dove, the more my visions increased, blessing me with an array of mystical encounters from spirit guides, powers animals, ancestors, arch angels and ascended masters, the faerie realm, ocean dwellers, and so on. Sometimes these mystical encounters would occur in my bath, sometimes during meditation, and most often while I was walking in nature. I also began hearing messages from people who had crossed over. This was incredibly surreal and, at times, frightening. In the beginning, I didn't understand what was happening, and I felt like I was on the brink of a complete mental breakdown.

Ed was supportive but from a distance. He didn't quite know what to do with me and tried his best to fix a situation that couldn't be fixed. My parents were also supportive and did their best to understand what I was going through. It was hard for them to grasp all the dramatic changes that were happening, especially after I announced I wanted to change my name to Beauty. I had been experiencing numerous visions of a woman named Beauty Indigo Blue: a Lemurian mystical goddess of light, keeper of the crystal caves, and an osmetic (a healer through osmosis, primarily with sound). At first, I thought she was my spirit guide. As the visions intensified, I realized she was more than a spirit guide; she was showing me I was her in a past life. She was asking me to alter my life situation by calling myself Beauty, so I could raise my vibration, hence, *The frequency of this name will heal you*. She also guided me to sound the pain within my body by using my voice as an instrument.

These dreamlike, yet lucid, present-moment experiences were the final push that motivated me to contact Topaz, the Reiki master my chiropractor mentor had advised me to call. Meeting her was a game changer. She helped me make sense of what was happening and guided me in the right direction, specifically to Beauty Indigo Blue, past lives, Lemuria, and something called a spontaneous Kundalini awakening. Her initial recommendation for me was to receive four consecutive sessions and go from there. After the four sessions were complete, I continued to see her on a regular basis. I then signed up for her level 1 Reiki class, in April 1999, and level 2, six months later in October.

As my soul-awakening journey continued, I felt a strong pull to write about my experiences. At first, the writing was for my own healing, until I began waking up every morning at three a.m. needing to write. This was when I realized I was also meant to share my story with others. In 2001, I wrote a book called *Within I Found Beauty*, and printed 150 copies. I gave most of them away at a show I produced called "Drama Queen 818," and the rest to family and friends.

For the next ten years, I dove into the alternative non- traditional medicine world. I studied and dabbled in a multitude of religious teachings, philosophies, and energy-based modalities. I signed up for every self-healing, transformational, wellness class/seminar that came my way. I fell in love with numerology/sacred geometry, travelled to sacred sites to heal my soul, cried every day for two years, and detoxed the crap out of my body. This wild, cleansing, healing ride led me to create a home business called Beauty's Healing Haven, through which I offered Reiki, soul-song Reiki, soul-song ceremonies (for loved ones who had crossed over), sound healing, chakra clearing/toning, crystal healing, and spiritual counseling. I also began spontaneously writing songs, practicing yoga, drumming, and offering workshops, called Healing Voice ~ Dancing Spirit. A few years after opening Beauty's Healing Haven, I was guided to create a new business called Beauty's Rainbow Productions (BRP). As my new business flourished, I made the difficult choice to let go of Beauty's Healing Haven and only offered sessions privately and distantly when time allowed. The decision to let go of BHH and focus on BRP gave me the opportunity to fully resurrect the drama queen I'd buried inside.

During this incredible, life-altering process, I dove deeper into my truth and began making decisions based on that truth. I was no longer willing to conform to the status quo. This monumental decision gave me the opportunity to uncover my own disempowering thoughts/beliefs within my subconscious mind and to focus on empowering thoughts instead. I knew, with this, I could raise my mind's vibration, which was essential to the new mindset I wanted to create. I was forty-two and in the best shape of my life mentally, physically, emotionally, and spiritually. My career was blazing forward, I was thriving, and to top it all off, LeRae was ready to join me.

WHAM!

No more singing, dancing, laughing, smiling, socializing, or love-making for me. I felt my heart shatter into trillions of pieces and the soul of my womb die, as I watched the child I gave birth to wither away.

What I haven't shared yet, is how equally devastating it was to leave Austin, my son. He was ten years old when LeRae was admitted to the hospital. He came home from school on October 19, 2006, to an empty house. He learned of LeRae's fate later that evening. Even though I knew his heart was breaking, I continued to reassure him she was going to be okay. One evening, Austin and I shared a beautiful, vulnerable moment as he began asking me questions about what was happening to his sister. His final question was, "Is she going to die?" I wrapped my arms around him and held him tightly, while I poured my love into him. I closed my eyes, and a vision appeared. It was LeRae. She was riding ten thousand wild horses across the midnight sky, and they were bringing her home. I started to cry and so did Austin. I was crying with joy, and he was releasing his grief. As I reflect, I realize he went down with LeRae—down his own healing path, burying his feelings, and basically raising himself for two years, while LeRae recovered from GBS. By the time Ed and I were fully available, he was transitioning into his teens.

I remember welcoming this new phase in his life with open arms. I was feeling vibrantly alive, more grateful than ever, and celebrating the gift of life. Every moment after LeRae came home from the hospital became one glorious blessing after another. I had given all my sacred objects away, except for LeRae's Raggedy Ann doll, the gold cross, and the rose quartz pyramid. This gave me the opportunity to continue practicing conscious thought, pure intention, and laser-like focus. I was no longer phased by life's challenges and instead, I simply blessed everything and everyone with love and light, just like I was guided to do in the hospital. I truly believed that, after my profound experience with LeRae, I could just sit back and live the rest of my life in bliss. Unbeknownst to me, lingering just below the surface was another life-altering experience.

BRP was in full swing again. I was preparing for an upcoming show, when I felt an unsettling feeling stir up inside me. It lasted only a few moments. A few weeks after the show, our family flew to Las Vegas for a holiday. On the last day, while sitting on a bench, waiting for my family to return from their roller coaster ride, the same unsettling feeling moved through me. Suddenly, I was outside of my body looking down at myself. I realized, I was being shown I was about to embark on another major transformation. Sure enough, the moment I arrived home, my transformation began. At first, it was subtle and slow, then came the flashbacks. They were vivid and intense. All the feelings I had suppressed during LeRae's GBS journey surfaced, as a virtual replay in my mind. These emotions magnified shortly after Austin's fifteenth birthday, the same age LeRae was when she was diagnosed with GBS. I knew he was moving into an important phase in his life, and I hoped it would give him the opportunity to tap into some of his own suppressed emotions. The kicker was, I was doing the same thing. Eventually, my euphoric, blissful state evaporated into a heavy cloud of fear, and I basically scared myself into an anxiety disorder that catapulted me into a deep depression. My loving, airy, light, and magical thoughts shockingly turned into an out-of-control fearful mindset

The medical terminology for what I experienced is post-traumatic stress disorder. I call it, my beautiful depression. It was surreal and somewhat scary, yet mysteriously tranquil. I also felt protected. At first, I wanted to deal with my beautiful depression holistically and on my own. "I'm a healer. I can heal myself" was my inner mantra. As time passed, I realized my limited thinking was keeping me from receiving the help I needed. I had reverted to an old way of thinking, with which I'd created a fearful belief about taking prescription medication. As long I wasn't the one taking the medication, everything was good. I thought I had transcended that belief while LeRae was in the hospital, I was mistaken.

After another long day of trying to heal myself on my own, I asked Ed to drive me to St. Paul's Emergency. I was sitting in the waiting room, paralyzed with fear and unable to catch my breath, when I realized, it had been five years since LeRae's diagnosis with GBS. Miraculously, a continuous, loving grace washed over me—the same feeling that washed over me when I heard,

Close your eyes. Close your eyes. Plant your feet. Plant your feet, while LeRae was choking uncontrollably in the emergency room. This time I heard, *It is time. It is time.*

"Holy moly," I whispered. "It's my time to heal."

I knew I needed to make a choice: become proactive and fight for my life or do nothing and die, likely from starvation—my physical body had become emaciated from the non-stop fight-or-flight response which was suppressing my appetite. I remember closing my eyes and allowing myself to feel the grace wash over me. An indescribable feeling of gratitude effortlessly weaved into the grace, forming an infinity symbol within my mind's eye. I was reminded of how precious life is and how living it through my physical body was more than a blessing; it was an incredible gift. Even in my darkest moments, I was being shown that the physical body is a temple. It holds within it a living light, and only through this sacred temple can living light truly shine.

"Oh my God," I blurted out, as images of LeRae, Austin, Ed, and my entire family flashed through my mind. These were followed by images of friends, acquaintances, people I'd never met, and, finally, all life. I saw how every living thing is a precious piece of the whole, and how nothing would exist without each piece following its own unique soul blueprint. Tears of joy trickled down my face. Yes, I want to live! Yes, I want to fight! I also knew this kind of fight had nothing to do with physical fighting. It would be heart centred, spirit driven, and soul powered. It would be unstoppable. LeRae had shown me this.

By the time the doctor came in to examine me, my symptoms were gone which was a surreal and confusing experience, until I heard, *You are already healed. Tell your story anyway.* Thankfully, I understood. I was being guided to tell the doctor the story about my beautiful depression, so I could continue playing out my human experience, and receive the blessings from within it. Near the end of my story, the doctor reached into his pocket and pulled out a pad of paper and a pen. When I was done talking, he handed me a prescription for Ativan. This was when I realized how deeply imbedded my limiting belief was. I thought there was no way I was going to take that or any kind of toxic medication. Then I heard, *Toxic? Is it toxic? Or is it simply a synthetic form of healing? Serving a purpose for whoever chooses to take it. Give thanks for your healing before you are healed.*

Remember, remember, remember, everything is meaningless until a meaning is given.

The moment I walked through my front door my symptoms returned. I immediately called Tillie with my concern regarding taking the medication. My conversation with her was brief: "Beauty, take the damn pills!" she lovingly commanded. She reassured me that everything was going to be okay and, if I chose to take the medication, she would help balance the medication with my body through a BodyTalk technique.

"Okay," I hesitantly replied, as I hung up the phone.

Everything changed when I let go of my toxic thoughts in taking the Ativan and the anti-depressant my family doctor had prescribed weeks earlier. I began a new powerful mantra, *thank you for my healing*, each time I took my medication. As I've mentioned, this experience was completely different than the one I had when I was thirty-three. During that time, I was unaware that my thoughts, feelings, and beliefs were directly related to my despairing situation or that we are all living light embodying a human form. I was also unaware of alternative options. I was simply living life through my conditioned thirty-three-year-old mindset and playing it out perfectly.

This time, I was all wings and no roots. I wasn't looking for a way out of my body, I was looking for a way back in. If I was going to have any chance of pulling myself out of my beautiful depression, I needed to plant my feet and root myself again.

At first, I could see how shocking it was for LeRae and Austin to see me in such a vulnerable, suppressed, and depressed state. Neither had seen me like that before. I did my best to let them know I was okay, even though I didn't appear to be. I told them I wasn't afraid and that I could feel God's love and God's grace surrounding me. I also expressed how loving myself with compassion was going to be the key to my recovery and that my profound love for them would be the driving force.

On the other hand, my parents and my husband Ed had witnessed me in a similar state when I was thirty-three. This time, my parents were more grounded and less afraid. They both rose to the occasion by offering unconditional love, support, and the space I needed to heal. They frequently checked in on me and offered their loving insight when I asked for it. My husband Ed was the big surprise. He literally championed me back into life, by gently and assertively asking me, every day, to go outside. Even though I felt divinely protected, I also felt profoundly exposed, as if I had no skin. The thought of venturing outside took my breath away and left me frozen in place. Our home had become my safe space. As I faithfully took the medication, I began feeling less exposed, more relaxed, and less afraid. I was finally able to accept Ed's request. At first, I could only walk to the end of our street and back. Gradually, with Ed's persistent support, together, we made our way around the block and eventually around the river. His commitment to seeing me through my beautiful depression gave me the confidence and the motivation to finally ask other people for help. Many of them have written in this book.

I knew from my own experience and from witnessing LeRae rise from death's door, that rebuilding my physical body and gaining weight was essential. Feeding my body with wholesome foods loaded with calories was the first step. Quieting my mind through stillness, reflection, and mindful meditation was next. Feeling my suppressed emotions, releasing them, and surrendering my will to divine will was the final step that gave me the precious peace I was looking for.

Everything shifted. A new hot yoga studio opened, and I signed up on the first day. I was able to ground my energy back into my body and release most of my tears. I practiced hot yoga for 101 days, and, on the 102nd day, I woke up to *The river is calling.* I began walking around the river on my own, which reminded me to go with the flow. At night I sat on the floor in my bathroom, shut the lights off, and practiced my breathing exercises. When winter came, I was guided to begin practicing Kundalini yoga at a nearby studio. There, I found my strength, endurance, and stamina. Around the same time, I participated in a meditation practice at a whimsical little flower shop that transformed into a sacred temple at night. The meditation practice was facilitated by a friend I'll affectionately call The Shoeless Sage. This was when I reconnected to the primordial songs of the Gregorian monks, sacred sound, and my own healing voice.

One morning, at three a.m., I woke up to the words, *Stop everything you are doing and just be. Remember, remember, remember, all you need is within you. The solace you seek is within. Your church is within.* I stopped all my practices and gave my body the time it needed to integrate the radical healing I had just immersed it in. A few months later, as I was leaving a massage therapy clinic, I heard, *Time to cut your hair*. I looked to the left and saw a hair salon next door. I walked in and asked if anyone was available to cut my hair.

"Yes, that would be me," the male hairstylist cheerfully said, "Someone just called and cancelled."

I hopped into his chair, "Do whatever you want," I confidently said.

I left the salon feeling magnificent. When I arrived home, I immediately showed LeRae. She was shocked and instantly cried. The last time I had cut my long hair off was when I was pregnant with her, and she'd never seen me with short hair. She walked over and gave me a big hug. "I love it," she joyfully said.

A few weeks later, I was back in his chair asking him to shave one side of my head and keep the other side as it was. He was more than willing to accommodate the radical change I was looking for. I felt empowered, free, and twenty years lighter.

Feeling stronger and more grounded in my body, I decided to attend the annual Body Soul and Spirit expo in Saskatoon. There, I experienced my first face reading and it was remarkably accurate. I decided to attend the seminar the following evening. The facilitator had a fiery personality and was passionately aligned with the information she was sharing, compelling me to sign up for the psychosomatic course she spoke about. I didn't realize it was hours from Saskatoon, in Biggar, until after I finished paying for it. This meant I would be away from home for the duration of the course.

The course was intense—filled with profound wisdom, practical exercises, and people who were open to new possibilities and seeking a clear vision to elevate their lives. It was also the place where I unknowingly stopped taking my prescription medication. The workshop had ended, and I was rummaging through my suitcase, looking for my keys. I reached into the side pocket and felt the prescription bottle sitting at the bottom. Suddenly, I realized I hadn't taken any of my pills. *You no longer need to take these.* I took a long deep breath, closed my eyes, and gave thanks for another miracle. My drive home was full of laughter, tears, soul songs, and thought-provoking words:

What you think of others, you think of yourself. What you think of yourself, you think of others. What others think of you is none of your business. Choose your thoughts and words wisely. You receive the energy of what you think and what you say first, then it ripples out to everything around you. Check yourself.

You were swept away in the sea of fear and the ocean of no motion. The fog came over your mind. You became the fear, instead of allowing its energy to flow through you. This is the way of the human—to rise and fall, to forget and remember, to be lost and be found. When your false voice becomes louder than your true voice, be kind to yourself and be kind to others. Everyone is on their own journey.

The fog has lifted. You are remembering who you are. The creator of your life. You have the power to choose what to think, feel, and believe. No one can do that for you unless you let them. You affect the All, and the All can only affect you when you allow it. Reclaim your sovereign voice.

The time has come to enjoy the fruits of life and the fruits of your labour. The time has come to have fun and play. Fill your life with trinkets, toys, and tools that are aligned with your soul's energy. You will know, by the way you feel, whether you love them or like them. Go for the love and let the rest go.

Everything is energy, and everything has a voice. Give your feelings a voice and listen to the whisperings of your soul.

Become a miracle thinker, and lead with your soul.

"Yes, become a miracle thinker and lead with my soul," I joyfully cried out.

As soon as I arrived home I wrote down all the thought-provoking words I received.

I was excited and eager to see what new adventure was coming my way. Initially, I was guided to offer healing sessions again and sing soul songs with my new drum; however, there was a quickening stirring within me that I couldn't shake. Would I record another album, produce another show, or open a wellness centre? I had so many options to choose from, so I asked for clarity.

"God, what is the highest calling for my life at this time?"

None of the above.

I found myself working full-time as the office manager for the family business my father opened in 1969. Ed started working there at age sixteen and, in 2009, he took over the business. In 2013, the current office manager moved to another province, and Ed needed to fill the position promptly. I agreed to step in with the clear intention that it was temporary. I had been working there off and on since I was twelve, and strongly felt I had already put in my time. While I'm thankful for the skills I obtained, I knew there was a greater calling for my life than sitting in an office all day. To top it off, the office was a male-dominated, eight-to-five, "let's get 'er done" work environment with Ed driving the train. My job was to manage the train.

A few months passed, and I was still working full-time and doing my best to manage the business and my husband. I quickly found out how challenging my task was going to be as I entered into a prosperous, lucrative business that thrived primarily on disorganized chaos. I honoured my feelings and had a meltdown.

"This, this is my life's highest calling? This has to be a mistake," I tearfully asked, crying out as I banged my hands on the desk with frustration.

> *There are no mistakes. You are exactly where you are supposed to be. When you were thirty-three, you were sitting in the pocket of doing. When LeRae came home from the hospital, you were sitting in the pocket of being. The basis of health is balance: balance between being and doing, doing and being. Root yourself in the soil of your soul, the womb of your existence. Centre yourself in the heart of inner knowing and cosmically connect to all that is. Root, centre, connect. This is your new practice. Sit, and be with, what makes you feel the most uncomfortable and love it anyway. Be grateful for everything and become the gratitude you speak of. Life is the meditation, step into it.*

Four years passed, and I continued to work at the family business, offer healing sessions when I was called to and write this book with LeRae. On October 18, 2017, I woke up feeling immensely grateful and equally overwhelmed. I met with LeRae.

"Oh my gosh, LeRae, I don't know if this book will ever be done. I have so much more to share that I can hardly handle it. All the blessings, mystical insights, and life-changing experiences continue to swirl around in my head. How are we ever going to finish this book if the stories keep coming?"

"Mom, just write another book," she simply said.

Laughing hysterically, I joyfully replied, "I can do that."

On December 22, 2017, I was relaxing in my favourite chair in the living room, and Ed was watching a football game on TV. Suddenly, I heard, *Time to ask Ed to write his closing story.* I quickly stood up, picked up the laptop, and sat back down in my chair. I turned towards him and pleasantly said, "This would be a great time to close your story."

"Sure," he said, as he put his coffee cup down on the table.

"Well," I said, giggling, "What have you learned since 2006 that you would like to share? I know it's been a long time. I just need to write a few things down."

Before he had a chance to answer, I jumped out of my chair, grabbed my mom's notes out of my purse, and quickly sat back down.

"Oh my God, it was December 22, 2006, when LeRae came home from the hospital for Christmas in a wheelchair. Do you know how amazing it is that I'm asking you at this exact moment to close your story! I love it," I said, crying joyfully.

Ed smiled as I asked him a different question, "So, how did it feel to have her come home that day? Let's start there."

He put his hands over his face and pondered my question for a few moments.

"Are you alright?" I asked.

He didn't answer. Finally, he took his hands away from his face, and I could see his eyes were filled with tears.

"Are you crying?" I curiously asked.

He was silent.

"You are!" I said with surprise. "Are they happy tears?"

"No," he replied. "I was remembering how awesome it was to have her home for Christmas and then how hard it was to get her here."

I stood up, threw myself onto the couch, and hugged him tightly. "That's okay. This says it all, there is nothing more you need to remember."

Thirteen
Holistic Embodiment

Beauty

I knew LeRae needed to work with practitioners who were willing to "tune into her," who had a clear sense of when to continue and when to stop—practitioners who were willing to go the distance by doing what was necessary to assist her in realigning her body, mind, and spirit, even when she was experiencing pain. LeRae attracted this into her life beautifully.

BodyTalk, by Tillie Dyck

BodyTalk works, first, by identifying the weak energy circuits that exist within the body. The practitioner then relies on the innate wisdom of the body to locate the energy circuits that need repair by using a form of biofeedback, which is a subtle muscle-testing technique. BodyTalk can be used to address specific diseases and disorders; it can be used as a means of prevention to keep the body in good health and can also be used to complement other treatment modalities.

Western Reiki, Jikiden Reiki, by Carol Dawson

LeRae began receiving continuous Reiki the moment she was admitted to the hospital. This was facilitated through Topaz and Beauty. She also received Theta Healing. Beauty asked me to share my knowledge regarding these two modalities, since I have practiced and taught both. I was happy to comply.

Reiki is Soul Energy or Life Force Energy that assists a person's body in healing and balancing all aspects of the mind, body, and spirit.

I originally studied Western Reiki and became a master. Years later, I was introduced to Jikiden Reiki and I was intrigued. *Jikiden* translates to "traditionally passed down" or "original and authentic." Nothing has been added or amended to the original teachings of founder Mikao Usui, which were originally called *Usui Reiki Ryoho* (*Ryoho* means "treatment method"). Chiyoko Yamaguchi and her son Tadao call this *unaltered Reiki* to differentiate it from the Western styles. Once I learned of original Reiki, I knew I needed to learn what the differences were. I immediately started training and pursued my teacher's certification. I studied Jikiden Reiki, under Tadao Yamaguchi, and trained to be a Shihan, which means *teacher* in Japanese. I have taught both Shoden (level 1), which focuses on healing and balancing the physical body, and Okuden (level 2), which provides the participant with the tools they need to heal psychological issues.

A Jikiden Reiki practitioner is taught to rest their hands gently on a person's body to feel for blockages and detect the byosen, which indicates toxic buildup in an area from trauma, injury, or disease. The practitioner will remain in the area until the byosen has subsided. Receiving a Jikiden Reiki treatment has many beneficial effects that include relaxation and feelings of peace, security, and wellbeing. It also relieves pain, reduces inflammation, releases toxins, and assists the body in healing much quicker. Many people have reported miraculous results. Babies and children are highly receptive to this healing energy. It is also beneficial for animals and plants.

In my experience, Western Reiki tends to focus more on the spiritual component of the person, and, in some cases, the hands do not touch the body when doing a treatment. I have found the benefits to be similar, since both Western Reiki and Jikiden Reiki recognize that the Reiki energy comes from a universal source and that it, not the practitioner, does the healing: the practitioner is simply a conduit to transmit the energy.

I met Beauty in October of 2012. We rented a big old house with a few other ladies, while we were taking a psychosomatic workshop together. One evening, after the workshop activities were complete, Beauty and I were sharing information about our lives while sitting around the dining room table. I told her I taught Jikiden Reiki and proceeded to explain how important it was for me to teach others that they can heal themselves, so they no longer have to depend on others.

Beauty

LeRae was six years old when she received her first Reiki treatment and around ten when I began encouraging her to be attuned to Reiki. Her response was always the same, "I'll think about it."

Astonishingly, during the same Reiki treatment when LeRae said she wanted to write a book about her experience with GBS, she also said she wanted to be attuned to Reiki. To hear her say those words was surprising and exhilarating.

"Which Reiki do you want to be attuned to? Traditional Western Reiki or Jikiden Reiki?" I asked excitedly.

"Jikiden," she said, with a smile.

"Okay, I'll send out an email tomorrow morning."

The following morning, I wrote to Dolphyn and Carol, asking if they were offering Jikiden Reiki courses. As I was about to press send, I was compelled to scroll through my emails instead. Carol's email was at the top. I opened it, read the content, and laughed out loud. It was perfect. She was offering a Shoden level 1 Jikiden Reiki course the following month. LeRae contacted Carol shortly after and signed up for the course. She completed her Shoden level 1 Jikiden Reiki course on August 18, 2013, which solidified her commitment towards her goal of making a full recovery by utilizing her own universal self-healing energy.

Theta Healing, by Carol Dawson

Theta Healing is a powerful technique that combines science and spirituality to identify and instantly transform deeply held blocks, negative beliefs, and trauma in the unconscious mind. As Theta Healers, we use the theta brainwave to help our clients change their belief system by connecting to divine energy. Their memories or experiences remain; only the limiting beliefs are changed. Through Theta Healing, we teach the person that letting go of whatever is causing their sickness or symptoms is safe to do. We can also assist in relieving any physical or psychological issue.

There are five major frequencies in the human brain: gamma, beta, alpha, theta, and delta. The theta brainwave is dominant during deep meditation, drifting to sleep, or hypnosis. Scientists have discovered that the theta brain frequency alleviates stress, reduces anxiety, facilitates deep relaxation, improves mental clarity and creative thinking, reduces pain, promotes euphoria, and provides access to instant healings. During Theta Healing sessions, the practitioner accesses the theta-wave state. While in this state, the practitioner can work directly with Source, Spirit, the Universe, God, or Creator of All That Is (depending on the person's spiritual and religious beliefs) to facilitate powerful healings.

During a Theta Healing session, the practitioner will identify which key beliefs are holding the physical or emotional issue in place. This will be done intuitively and through a process called *digging*. Digging is a technique used to work down through the layers of beliefs to uncover the bottom/root or key belief. When a key belief is transformed, the beliefs stacked above it will automatically change, instantly freeing the person from their limiting patterns.

The practitioner determines whether the person is holding certain beliefs by using muscle testing. This technique will also validate that a belief has shifted. Most issues can be addressed with one or two sixty to ninety-minute sessions; however, some may take longer. Theta Healing works only with the informed consent of the person. The practitioner will create a safe and supportive space in which the person can explore any area of their life they would like to make changes to.

In addition to improving health and wellbeing, a person can work on anything, from finding their most compatible soulmate, to unlocking their creativity, growing their business, and creating wealth and abundance, increasing confidence and self-esteem, releasing fears and phobias, addictions, healing trauma, disease or disorders, etc.

Theta Healing is a gentle process and requires no reliving of past traumas. The possibilities are endless!

A Shaman, by Trent Deerhorn

A shaman is a harmonizer. There are many different types and traditions within shamanism. I have been trained by many different shamans over the years and consider myself to be an eclectic-style shaman. Part of what I do is energy work. The other part involves journeying to different realms to find answers and medicines to help in the healing of the person I am working with. When I say *medicines*, I am not talking about pharmaceuticals. I am talking about the things that help people on their spirit journey on this earth walk, right here and right now. I can also see various outcomes of proposed actions. This is like looking through a kaleidoscope of possibilities and choosing which one will lead to the most beneficial outcome for all concerned. I also talk to earth-bound spirits, help them into the light, and work with soul retrieval.

Often, to do soul retrieval, I must journey to where the soul energy is residing. It could be a place, or with a particular person, in limbo, or in another dimension. I could write an entire book about how to journey, but, suffice to say, journeying allows me to access many realms through the art of trance and travel in combination with one another. There are many ways that I can induce the journey. I usually sit quietly and go into a trance or softly drum while going into my inner stillness. Then the journey begins.

To understand soul retrieval, one must first grasp the concept of what we mean by *soul* and *spirit*. In shamanism, we do not necessarily think of those two terms as interchangeable. We tend to define them as different forms of energy. The spirit of an individual is that which is eternally connected to Spirit/God/Goddess and is impervious to all harm. Through lifetimes, the soul energy, which incarnates in order to evolve into spirit energy, learns and grows through earthly experiences. We can have many soul energies residing within one body or *temple*.

Sometimes, through traumas, illnesses, accidents, injuries, etc., the soul energy becomes more primal and more fragile than the spirit energy and can even step out of the temple for a quick "coffee break." Most of the time, when the soul energy steps out, it immediately steps back into the temple after the break. It then continues on its path of learning and growing to become spirit energy. Sometimes, the soul energy becomes attached to someone or something else in the process, quite by accident, or even becomes earth bound to a place (for example, where a particular trauma has occurred). Even a heated argument can result in *soul loss* or, worse yet, *soul oppression*. This is when one person's strong soul energy invades their opponent in an argument, or in a battle for the purpose of using their will power to weaken and control the opponent. This is unhealthy for both opponents, because the one whose soul is oppressed is now carrying around someone else's soul energy, like a baby grand piano on their back. The one who did the oppressing has been immediately weakened by the loss of their soul energy.

When this is experienced, it is time to see a shaman. They will be able to assist in the retrieval of the soul energies, heal the ones that have been oppressed, and extract the soul energies of those who have invaded the energy field (either on purpose or inadvertently). When the extraction takes place, the soul energies are then sent into the light for healing, so they can spontaneously return in the proper time, place, and space for that temple.

Beauty

Even though LeRae made a miraculous recovery in the hospital, she needed to continue her rehab exercises and post-care regimen at home. This was crucial if she wanted to achieve her goal of a full recovery. In support of LeRae and her goal, doctors referred her to numerous rehab facilities and physiotherapy clinics. In the beginning, she spent many weeks at City Hospital, mostly in the pool—she loved the pool. The pool exercises were instrumental in helping her regain the strength in her legs, and, eventually, she was fitted for below-the-knee leg braces. She wore the leg braces for many months, until she was strong enough to walk without them.

Walking with LeRae before GBS was more like running a race—the faster the better. After GBS, in the early days, when she was learning how to walk again, walking was slow. Every step she took was executed with great focus and willful intent. I felt like I was walking a sacred pilgrimage alongside an earth angel, where her every step was enveloped with grace and gratitude. The more we walked, the stronger she became. Eventually, walking became second nature for her. Running, however, was out of the question. Her ankles were weak and the nerves in her right big toe were continuing to regenerate, which meant that if she tried to run she would fall.

It was her tenacious, persistent personality that helped her push through the pain during rehabilitation and which continues to help her to this day. She also continued following a holistic care regimen, which elevated her post-rehabilitation experience to another level.

Nutritional support, reflexology, and chiropractic care were only a handful of the many modalities that helped LeRae with her recovery.

Nutritional Support, by Dolphyn Boschman

Beauty contacted me when LeRae was able to eat on her own again. She wanted to know what I would recommend to help her recover faster, gain weight, and begin detoxing the medications LeRae was taking. I work exclusively with Sunrider Whole Foods for my nutritional toolbox, and I knew their products would be key in LeRae's recovery. All Sunrider products are created in concert with the philosophy of regeneration. Simply put, when you nourish and cleanse the body with the right combination of foods, the body will find its own inherent balance.

Sunrider foods are formulated and concentrated to help the body regenerate. They are easy to digest and made from food-grade plants. Below are the products that I recommended to assist LeRae in her recovery:

1. NuPlus and VitaShake help rebuild muscle and bone tissue. These foods, called *angel's porridge* in ancient times, provide the building

blocks of cells. They are made from predigested grains, beans, and vegetables, making the products easy to digest. They are often used as Pablum for babies or adult "baby food." Beauty would find creative ways to ensure LeRae received these nutrients, such as secretly mixing them into LeRae's DQ Blizzards, which LeRae ate for extra calories.

2. VitaDophilus is a stabilized acidophilus mixed with apple. The apple allows the probiotic to pass through the stomach acids intact and reach the small intestine, where the friendly bacteria is needed to help digest food. Beauty added this to everything.

3. VitaSpray is a complete B vitamin with extra B12. It is a food-grade source; therefore, the body recognizes it as food and is thus absorbed fully into the body. The spray was easy for LeRae to administer under the tongue and she loved the taste.

4. Calli tea is an ancient formula to nourish the brain and kidneys and detox cells. Calli can bind to heavy metals and other toxins. This helped LeRae eliminate toxins from the medication in her body. She would drink it cold, which was easier for her to consume.

Another product Beauty used was Egyptian Magic All Purpose Skin Cream. Egyptian Magic is an all-natural skin cream made from six powerful healing ingredients: olive oil, beeswax, honey, bee pollen, royal jelly and bee propolis. Beauty and Ed would massage LeRae with it every day to keep her muscles loose and, as a result, her skin was like silk, despite all the medications she was on, and she had no bed sores! The medical staff would comment on how beautiful LeRae's skin looked.

Reflexology, by Jackie Jenson

I am a holistic health practitioner with training in several modalities, including reflexology. In my experience, reflexology has proven to be effective at relieving the underlying stress of many imbalances. Our physical being, when given the proper circumstances, is adept at rejuvenating and restoring optimal health.

The science of reflexology is based on the principle that there are reflex areas in the feet and hands that correspond to every organ, gland, and system of the body. A reflexologist uses their thumb and fingers to stimulate these reflex areas. The main benefits of reflexology include a reduction in stress and tension, improved blood circulation, the unblocking of nerve impulses, and a restoration of homeostasis or balance in the body. An average session with a reflexologist lasts approximately forty-five minutes, during which time all the reflex areas on each foot receive attention. Our feet connect us to the earth. Reflexology is an excellent way to keep the pathways open and energy flowing through the entire body.

My friend Beauty called to book a session for LeRae. She said she received an intuitive message that LeRae needed to see me regarding issues she was having with digestion and elimination.

Beauty and LeRae arrived the following day for the appointment. While Beauty shared pertinent information about LeRae's present circumstance, I asked LeRae to sit in the reclining lounge chair. When Beauty was finished, she exited the healing room. I walked over to LeRae and sat down in front of her. I reached down and picked up the hot towels I had prepared for her prior to her arrival. I wrapped her feet with the hot towels while I asked her what was going on in her life. The soles of the feet are like a map of the entire body to a reflexologist. We take note of any areas with sensitivity, tenderness, or tension. During a session, the entire foot, top and bottom, including the lower leg, is worked on. In LeRae's case, I took extra time stimulating the reflexes on the feet that are related to the entire digestive system. This included the ascending, transverse, and descending colons. I noticed a degree of tenderness and congestion in that area, so I gently worked on it throughout the course of the treatment. Overall, LeRae appeared more relaxed by the end of the session.

As a general intuitive with in-depth experience in meditation, yoga, and energy work, I tend to infuse sessions with deep awareness, especially when multiple existing physical conditions have an emotional/mental stress and trauma component linked to the condition. The moment there is a recognition or expression of the related issue, the associated condition is relieved. Because of the extreme nature of LeRae's sudden illness, she had become dependent on others to support and care for her. Apparent during the session was that her body was holding onto things it needed to let go of.

She was ready to fully reclaim her health and independence in all areas of her life. As she acknowledged this, her physical body and her manifesting issue of constipation began flowing in a new direction. Beauty informed me a few days later that her symptoms were relieved.

I am grateful for the opportunity to have witnessed the love and dedication of LeRae's family towards her healing and am honoured to have been a part of it.

Beauty
Chiropractic Care

I was twenty-seven when I experienced my first chiropractic treatment. I was working as a medical office assistant and had sustained a minor neck injury while typing. Heather Paull, a vibrant, fun-loving chiropractor, had just moved her private practice onto the same floor where I worked. I decided to book an appointment. Her first treatment gave me instant relief, which motivated me to continue seeing her on a regular basis, during which time my neck injury healed, and we became friends.

Years later, I met Yancy during a sound-healing workshop, and I instantly felt a kindred connection with him. I didn't realize he was a chiropractor until a friend recommended I go see him. My friend said his method of treatment was unique and embodied a holistic approach unlike anything she'd experienced before. I booked my appointment with him the following day.

My initial appointment was just like my friend described, unlike anything I'd experienced before. It was exactly what I needed at that time, and I've continued to see Yancy, on and off, over the years. When LeRae was to begin her post-trauma rehabilitation routine, I knew his healing touch would contribute significantly to her goal of making a full recovery. Initially, her visits, as she pushed through the pain, were frequent and emotionally exhausting. During adjustments of her toes, her pain became almost unbearable. She had stopped taking high doses of pain medication and needed to rely on her own coping skills. Breathing deeply and allowing her tears to flow helped her move through the pain with greater ease. Yancy was aware of the pain she was experiencing and did his best to ease her distress by being as gentle as possible. I watched him remain calm and uninhibited through LeRae's emotional turmoil, as he worked on her feet. I could see he was completely aligned with her body, mind, and spirit. He knew precisely when LeRae had reached her pain threshold and would ease off accordingly, which gave her time to relax her body. He also knew when she was ready to continue.

LeRae remembers her experience with Yancy as a painful one, especially when he adjusted her toes. Her exact words after a toe-adjustment session were, "I'm so glad he isn't afraid to crack my toes. I know he's waking them up, so they can heal." For this, she is grateful.

Mystical Magical Miracle #9

During LeRae's recovery, I spent most of my time ensuring all her needs were met, which, for me, meant putting most of my needs on hold. Everything changed after I received a clear message in the wee hours of the morning, telling me I needed to book an appointment with Yancy. I called his office that morning, and the receptionist told me he had a cancellation.

"Super, please pencil me in," I said happily.

While driving to the appointment, my chest began to ache. It was intense. It felt like my chest was caving in on itself, and, with each breath, the ache deepened. As I turned left, from Broadway onto 8th Street, I began crying hysterically.

"What's happening?" I asked out loud, sobbing as I placed my right hand over my heart.

A holographic image suddenly appeared in my mind's eye. It was my heart, shattered into trillions of pieces, with each shattered piece containing the sum of my whole heart. A warm tingling sensation rose from within the deep ache, and I knew something incredible was about to happen.

"Oh my God, he's going to help me build a new heart," I exclaimed as my hysterical crying turned into hysterical laughter.

By the time I parked my vehicle in front of the chiropractic office, I'd pulled myself together—at least, I thought so. The receptionist could see I'd been emotionally upset and quickly placed me in the treatment room. The moment she placed me in the room, I started crying again and by the time Yancy entered I was sobbing. Before he could say anything, I wrapped my arms around him and hugged him tightly. He was surprised and somewhat confused with my greeting until I shared my experience. He placed one hand on my shoulder and gestured towards the examining table with the other. I proceeded to lay down on my back and stare up at the ceiling.

"Breathe deeply," he calmly said. "It will help you relax."

I closed my eyes, placed both hands over my chest, and began breathing deeply. A few moments passed before he sat down on a chair next to me. He placed one hand over my hands and one on the top of my head. I felt an immense heat fill my chest. Tears began spontaneously trickling down the side of my face as a magnificent white light filled my heart centre. The immense heat transformed into a warm melting sensation methodically welding the shattered holographic pieces of my heart back together. A heart-shaped rainbow manifested from within the white light, and my new holographic heart was formed. Yancy slowly lifted his hands away from my body and asked if there was anything else he could do for me.

With immense gratitude, I tearfully replied, "Thank you. Thank you. Thank you."

His role in my own personal healing was incredibly profound and the reason why, when I see him publicly, my reaction is always the same: my heart fills with immense joy, tears well up in my eyes, and I hug him with deep gratitude.

Acknowledgements

Travis (physical therapist),

Thank you for carrying me through some of the most painful and difficult aspects of my recovery. From the moment we met, I knew you were going to push me past my comfort zone, test my limits, and do whatever was necessary to ensure I made a full recovery. Even when I was skin and bones, heavily medicated, and at my lowest, you still believed in me. You helped me rebuild my body, mind, and spirit and gave me the confidence and strength to walk again.

Thank you for giving me one hundred percent of yourself every day. You were always there for me, present in every moment, dedicating your time, energy and love. I will never forget what you did for me. I am eternally grateful.

Jennifer (recreation therapist),

I knew the moment you walked into my hospital room that you were going to make a difference in my life. With your bright eyes and inviting smile, you made me feel as though nothing was wrong and I was just a kid needing some fun in her life. You challenged me in the best way possible—through art, creativity, games, and laughter. My fine motor skills were non-existent, and my fingers were weak. Day after day, you worked to strengthen my hands through tedious tasks, until, finally, you brought me paint, paint brushes, and a wooden box. I was up for the challenge and determined to paint it myself. Even though my hands were shaking uncontrollably, and I had to spend almost an hour trying to paint just one small side, you sat with me, patiently, allowing me to do what I could until I asked for help. By the time I finished painting the box, my fine motor skills had improved, and the shaking had subsided. I could finally feed myself soup. Without your clever, fun, and creative ideas, I wouldn't have the strength to be doing the things I'm doing today.

Thank you for treating me with such kindness, respect, and love. You inspired me, every day, to go beyond what I thought I was capable of and to find the joy in every situation, which is why I chose to pursue a diploma in the field of Recreation Therapy. I will forever be grateful for the time we spent together. You showed me what true compassion is, and I strive to find that every day.

Thank you.

Jenn (occupational therapist),

I was so happy and relieved when you walked into my room with Travis that day. You became the second half of my dream team. I'm truly blessed to have had you by my side through all the painful and challenging exercises Travis had me do. You were the soft voice encouraging me and telling me I was strong enough. You were my rock, my cheerleader, and my steady hand to hold. Your inner spark inspired me and ignited my will to keep going.

Thank you for always knowing how to make me laugh. This is one of my favourite things about you. I felt you were like a friend to me, more than just my therapist, and I looked forward to seeing you every day. I'm eternally grateful for the genuine love and kindness you showed me. It will stay with me forever.

Healthcare workers,

To all the doctors, nurses, care aids, and paramedics, thank you for ensuring I received the best care possible and for doing whatever was necessary to keep me alive.

Thank you to the many therapists who always encouraged me to challenge myself, so I could return to my best life.

To the housekeeping staff, particularly the housekeeper who hung her Rosary above my bed while I was in recovery, thank you for your love and support.

Thank you to all the kitchen staff who brought my daily meals. I loved choosing what to eat each morning.

To the wonderful tutor who homeschooled me, both in the hospital and at home, until I was ready to go back to school, thank you.

A special thank you goes to all the blood donors. Without you, the IVIG treatment necessary for my recovery would be non-existent.

Healers,

I'm deeply honoured to have had you by my side in the fight for my life. Each one of you played a vital role in my recovery, especially in the beginning, when no one knew what I needed. With love and grace, you answered my call without hesitation, expecting nothing in return other than to see me well. Thank you for blessing me with your profound healing abilities.

Thank you to all the people who prayed for me. Every intention and feeling that you poured into those prayers reached me, giving me the strength and will to keep pushing forward. I am truly grateful.

To my dear friends,

I'm unbelievably grateful for the kindness, love, and compassion you showed me over those few months I was in the hospital. I imagine how difficult it must have been for you to see me in that state. You were with me all the way and you were there when I needed you the most, creating laughter in my heart and light within my soul. I cherished our precious moments long after you'd gone. I will always remember what you did for me and there will forever be a special place for you in my heart.

To my family,

Nana, thank you for taking such amazing care of me while I was in the hospital and for sitting by my side and reading stories that lifted my spirit. Your soothing voice calmed my nervous mind and made me feel safe. I'm so grateful to you for bringing my friends to visit me. I will treasure your selfless acts forever. The love you have for me and our family is limitless.

Papa, thank you for being a presence of strength in my life, opening yourself up to the unknown, and loving me dearly.

Uncle Curtis, Aunt Tami, and Zach, thank you for your loving thoughts, handmade gifts, and well-wishes. They warmed my heart and always put a smile on my face.

Grandma Helen, thank you for your love, support, and your willingness to help everyone, even in unpleasant moments. I am thankful to have you in my life.

Aunt Judy, thank you for your tender love, miracle prayers, and healing words.

Austin, thank you for your courage, thoughtful gifts, and unconditional love. You were so brave, strong, and willing to do whatever you could to brighten my day. I'm so grateful to have you as my brother.

Dad, as I write this, tears of gratitude are streaming down my face. Thank you for opening your heart and allowing your true nature to shine through. You showed me how deeply you care with the actions you took while I was in the hospital: researching every day, working to support our family, sitting by my side, and meeting with the doctors, even convincing them they were wrong about me. Through all the pain, you had so much love, more love than I could have ever imagined. You gave me strength, courage, and the will to never give up, to always keep going.

I always felt safe whenever you were near me, holding my hand and telling me everything was going to be okay. Thank you for standing by my side and being the best father I could have ever asked for.

Mom, you are the most supportive, intelligent, sacred, fun-loving soul in my life. You are a true gift to this world and to me. You helped give me the strength to live again. We always say that without the ventilator or medications I would've died, but we always forget one thing—you. Without you, I wouldn't still be living on this Earth.

You saved me. You listened and answered my call. You created a magnificent place for people to come and share their gifts—with you, with me, and our family. The love you've shown me is the greatest love I've ever experienced. There are no words to truly express how thankful I am for you. You are not only my mother; you are my mentor and my best friend. You are so good to me.

Thank you for this life.

I love you all.

Beauty

To my beloved family, extended family, friends, healers, and healthcare workers, thank you for everything you did to provide LeRae with a safe, loving, and gracious healing environment. To Travis, Jennifer, and Jenn, your commitment of seeing LeRae through the acute stage of her recovery was remarkable. I was honoured to be in your presence and to witness your unwavering dedication to her. Your genuine love for her touched me deeply.

To every person who prayed and held space for LeRae and our family, thank you.

In 2006, when LeRae was in PICU, one of the nurses and a few doctors asked me, "What are you doing?"

"Reiki," I replied.

"What is that?"

Their response was one of the reasons why I wrote this book. Thankfully, years later, many of the modalities mentioned, including Reiki, are finally being acknowledged and recognized as key factors in creating a more balanced healing experience.

I truly believe knowledge can be a powerful conduit for deeper understanding, and through deeper understanding, fear can move into faith, which gives birth to a new awareness by opening the door to an elevated mindset. An elevated mindset, along with a balanced healing experience makes room for divine grace to flow through and for love to guide the way.

Let love guide the way.

LeRae

If you are feeling hopeless, defeated, or have lost your way, this is what I want to say to you: I believe in you. Allow my belief in you to be the driving force that motivates you to take action until you are strong enough to believe in yourself. Rise up my friend, fight the battle within, with everything you have and surrender when it is time to surrender. Allow yourself to be reborn into a being that is capable of the impossible, because it is all possible. Say yes to every prayer, helping hand, and medical intervention that feels right for you. You are worthy of it all. You are brave and stronger than you know. You are a warrior.

Rise free with me.

Practitioners

Tillie Dyck is the creator and director of SageStone Wellness Centre. She is a registered massage therapist, a certified PaRama BodyTalk Practitioner (ParCBP), and a full member of The Natural Health Practitioners of Canada Association (NHPC). Website: www.sagestones.ca

Kellie Welk founded Earth Beat Drums in 1999.
Website: www.earthbeatdrums.com

Trent Deerhorn: Deerhorn Shamanic Services
Website: www.deerhornshamanic.com

T. Dolphyn Boschman has been a registered holistic health practitioner and massage therapist for over twenty years. She uses Sunrider Wholefood products, professionally and personally, for her nutritional toolbox and holistic lifestyle. Website: www.dolphyn.ca

Jackie Jenson: founder and CEO at Twig & Squirrel's Wild Goods, Saskatoon, SK.

Additional Modalities, Therapies, and Nutritional Support

Cranial sacral therapy - emotional freedom technique (EFT) – acupuncture – biofeedback therapy – access consciousness - massage therapy – essential oil/aromatherapy - music therapy - pet therapy - nature therapy art therapy - colour therapy – earthing - astrology - naturopathic medicine - ayurvedic medicine

The Yuen Method: Colette Stefan, Author of
The Truth is Funny, Shift Happens
Website: www.thetruthisfunny.com

Psychosomatic Therapy: Lorrel Elian, Creator and founder
of Passion to Profit and Your Emotional Mind
Website: www.lorrelelian.com

Vitajuwel: Jacqueline Neusch, Gemologist
Website: www.vitajuwel.ca

About the Authors

Beauty H. Faulkner was born and raised in Saskatoon, Saskatchewan. In 1997, her soul-awakening journey began, leading her to self-realization through deep study and devoted practice of alternative and energy medicine. She is passionate about the soul's evolution and helping others elevate their lives. She is a singer, song writer, recording artist, and the founder of Beauty's Rainbow Productions.

LeRae Faulkner was born and raised in Saskatoon, Saskatchewan. After overcoming a life-threatening illness, she began travelling the world, expressing her creativity and living life to the fullest. She also attended the college of Saskatchewan Polytechnic, graduating with honours and a diploma in therapeutic recreation. She has a passion for helping others, which motivated her to share this story and explore the possibility of becoming a writer.

To learn more about Beauty and LeRae, please
visit www.heartsoulanthology.ca